TARGET MATHS

Year 6

Stephen Pearce

Elmwood Press

© Stephen Pearce

First published 2002 by
Elmwood Press
80 Attimore Road
Welwyn Garden City
Herts. AL8 6LP
Tel. 01707 333232

Reprinted 2002, 2003, 2004, 2005, 2006, 2007, 2008, 2009, 2011

British Library Cataloguing in Publication Data

Pearce, Stephen

    1. Mathematics—1961–
    I. Title

    ISBN 1 902 214 242

Numerical answers are published in a separate book

Typeset and illustrated by Tech-Set Ltd., Gateshead, Tyne and Wear
Printed and bound by Bookwell.

PREFACE

Target Maths has been written for pupils in Year 6 and their teachers.

The intention of the book is to provide teachers with material to teach *all* the NNS objectives, as set out in the yearly teaching programme, and with *all* the children in their class able to work at their appropriate level of ability.

One of the key principles for the approach to teaching recommended by the NNS is 'controlled differentiation, with all pupils engaged in mathematics related to a common theme.' **Target Maths** is structured so that controlled differentiation is built into every lesson. How a teacher decides to use the material would depend upon the children's familiarity with the topic and the amount of time that is available.

Each lesson in the book is divided into four sections. The four sections are:

- The introduction: a clearly stated learning intention and, where necessary, explanations and examples of new work.
- Section A: activities based upon the NNS expected learning outcomes for Year 5 pupils. This section can be used to remind children of work previously covered, as well as providing material for the less confident child.
- Section B: activities based upon the NNS expected learning outcomes for Year 6 pupils. Most children should be able to work successfully at this level.
- Section C: This section provides extension material for the faster workers and for those who need to be moved quickly onto more challenging tasks. Problems in Section C can also provide useful material for discussion in the plenary session.

The correspondence of the three sections to the NNS learning outcomes expected of different year groups provides a simple, manageable framework for both the formal and informal assessment of children's progress. The expectations in the yearly teaching programmes correspond to these National Curriculum levels.

- Section A   Year 5   revision of level 3, but mainly level 4
- Section B   Year 6   consolidation of level 4, start on level 5
- Section C   Year 6   extension, mainly level 5

Both the NNS Teaching Programme for Year 6 and the Term Framework are in the Answer Book with **Target Maths** page references for all the NNS objectives.

The author is indebted to many colleagues who have assisted him in this work. He is particularly grateful to David Rayner and Sharon Granville for their invaluable advice and support.

CONTENTS

On this page you will learn:

- to multiply and divide whole numbers by 10, 100 and 1000.

Examples

×10	digits move 1 place to the left	134×10	$= 1340$
×100	digits move 2 places to the left	134×100	$= 13\,400$
×1000	digits move 3 places to the left	134×1000	$= 134\,000$
÷10	digits move 1 place to the right	$27\,000 \div 10$	$= 2700$
÷100	digits move 2 places to the right	$27\,000 \div 100$	$= 270$
÷1000	digits move 3 places to the right	$27\,000 \div 1000$	$= 27$

- to multiply and divide decimals by 10.

Examples

The same rules apply.

×10	digits move 1 place to the left	$1.7 \times 10 = 17$	$0.6 \times 10 = 6.0$
÷10	digits move 1 place to the right	$13 \div 10 = 1.3$	$2.0 \div 10 = 0.2$

A

Multiply by 10.

1. 38
2. 174
3. 200
4. 1368
5. 4520
6. 12 000

Divide by 10.

7. 7000
8. 820
9. 35 000
10. 700 000
11. 2050
12. 24 360

Multiply by 100.

13. 400
14. 92
15. 726
16. 1200
17. 3000
18. 10 000

Divide by 100.

19. 1900
20. 38 000
21. 450 000
22. 75 600
23. 2 000 000
24. 90 000

B

Write the answers only.

1. 1427×10
2. 164×100
3. $56\,400 \div 10$
4. $280\,000 \div 1000$
5. 1308×100
6. 1.4×10
7. $12.0 \div 10$
8. $164\,000 \div 100$
9. 310×1000
10. $2.6 \div 10$
11. 0.7×10
12. $9\,500\,000 \div 1000$
13. $327\,180 \div 10$
14. $38\,912 \times 10$
15. $56\,000 \div 100$
16. 42×1000

C

Copy and complete.

1. $\square \times 10 = 6.0$
2. $\square \div 10 = 3.0$
3. $\square \times 100 = 3\,040\,000$
4. $\square \div 100 = 2540$
5. $\square \times 1000 = 21\,000$
6. $\square \div 1000 = 500$
7. $\square \times 100 = 51\,000$
8. $\square \div 10 = 7.5$
9. $\square \times 10 = 42\,000$
10. $\square \div 100 = 3.2$
11. $\square \times 100 = 62$
12. $\square \div 100 = 0.8$
13. $\square \times 10 = 0.1$
14. $\square \div 1000 = 1291$
15. $\square \times 1000 = 1\,480\,000$
16. $\square \div 10 = 0.05$

ROUNDING

On this page you will learn to round numbers to the nearest whole one or to the nearest multiple of 10 and to use rounding to approximate calculations.

Examples

to the nearest 1	$19{\cdot}7 \div 3{\cdot}9 \rightarrow 20 \div 4 \rightarrow 5$
to the nearest 10	$329 + 264 \rightarrow 330 + 260 \rightarrow 590$
to the nearest 100	$638 \rightarrow 600, \quad 2351 \rightarrow 2400$
to the nearest 1000	$4835 \rightarrow 5000, \quad 13\,294 \rightarrow 13\,000$

A Round each of these numbers to the nearest:

(10)	(100)	(1000)	(10)	(100)	(1000)
1 288	**5** 743	**9** 4630	**13** 3799	**17** 4150	**21** 11 426
2 641	**6** 3450	**10** 7373	**14** 32	**18** 5838	**22** 549
3 67	**7** 1365	**11** 12 517	**15** 485	**19** 921	**23** 7802
4 365	**8** 216	**12** 5995	**16** 1843	**20** 2094	**24** 19 287.

B

Round these football crowds:
a) to the nearest 1000.
b) to the nearest 100.

1	Arsenal	38 051
2	Chelsea	34 646
3	Leeds	39 837
4	Liverpool	44 718
5	Manchester Utd.	67 581
6	Newcastle	51 625
7	Sunderland	45 078
8	Tottenham	34 453

Approximate by rounding to the nearest:

10

9 $248 + 373$
10 $542 + 267$
11 $638 - 294$
12 $762 - 357$
13 68×5
14 79×9
15 $158 \div 4$
16 $317 \div 8$

whole one

17 $6{\cdot}5 + 7{\cdot}3$
18 $18{\cdot}2 + 6{\cdot}7$
19 $20{\cdot}8 - 6{\cdot}3$
20 $43{\cdot}2 - 17{\cdot}8$
21 $6{\cdot}9 \times 3{\cdot}1$
22 $14{\cdot}6 \times 5{\cdot}1$
23 $12{\cdot}4 \div 2{\cdot}1$
24 $41{\cdot}6 \div 6{\cdot}9$

C

Estimate each of the following. Give your answer to the nearest 10, 100, 1000, 10,000, 100 000 or 1 000 000. Explain how you made each estimate.

1 pages in an encyclopaedia
2 people in the United Kingdom
3 children in your school
4 the distance to Rome in metres
5 days you have lived
6 people on a full bus
7 words in the Bible
8 children in a Secondary School
9 the capacity of a bath in millilitres
10 an adult's weight in grams
11 the length of the Thames in miles
12 miles to Australia

On this page you will learn to make and justify estimates.

A

Estimate the numbers shown by the arrows.

1  100   200

2  200   300

3 30   50

4 45   55

5 0   25

6 This bar line graph shows the percentage mark achieved by children in a test.

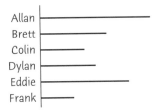

Allan got 100%.
a) Who got 50%?
b) Who got twice as many as Colin?
c) Who got half as many as Brett?
d) Estimate the mark achieved by each of the five boys.

B

Estimate the numbers shown by the arrows.

1 3000   4000

2 0   10000

3 −5   0

4 0   1

5 −25   0

6 Six friends ordered pizzas. When they had finished eating, their pizzas looked like this:

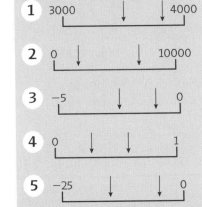

Estelle   Wendy   Jenny

Gill   Judy   Sharon

Who had eaten:
a) twice as much as Gill?
b) five times as much as Judy?
c) half as much as Sharon?

7 Estimate the proportion of each pizza which had been eaten as a percentage.

C

Estimate the numbers shown by the arrows.

1  5000   10000

2  0   2

3 −20   0

4 5   7.5

5 −50   0

6 Estimate the number of words in your reading book. Explain your method.

Use your method to estimate the number of words in:
a) a picture book
b) a dictionary
c) an encyclopaedia.

7 Estimate the number of times someone blinks in a day.
Explain your method.

On this page you will learn to recognise odd and even numbers and to give examples that match general statements about odd or even numbers.

An even number is a number which can be divided exactly by 2.
An odd number cannot be divided by 2 without leaving a remainder.

Examples

$34 \div 2 = 17$ 34 is an even number.

$35 \div 2 = 17$ remainder 1   35 is an odd number.

Give three examples for each of the following questions.
Is the answer odd or even:

1   if you subtract an odd number from an even number?

2   if you subtract an odd number from an odd number?

3   if you subtract an even number from an even number?

4   if you subtract an even number from an odd number?

B

Use each set of digits to make six 3-digit numbers.
For each question state how many of your numbers are odd and how many are even.

1 (2, 7, 4)   2 (5, 1, 9)   3 (7, 6, 3)   4 (6, 2, 8)

Give four examples for each of the following questions.

5   Is the product odd or even:
   a) if you multiply two even numbers?
   b) if you multiply two odd numbers?
   c) if you multiply an odd number and an even number?

C

Use these digits. | 1 | | 5 | | 2 | | 3 |

1   List all the four-digit odd numbers you can make.

2   List all the four-digit even numbers you can make.

Copy and complete these rules by writing 'odd' or 'even' in the box.

3   If you multiply three even numbers the answer is always [＿＿＿].

4   If you multiply three odd numbers the answer is always [＿＿＿].

5   If you multiply two odd numbers and one even number the answer is always [＿＿＿].

6   If you multiply two even numbers and one odd number the answer is always [＿＿＿].

7   Give four examples for each of the rules.

On these pages you will learn to recognise and order negative numbers.

Negative numbers
below zero
Have a minus sign

Positive numbers
above zero

−10 −9 −8 −7 −6 −5 −4 −3 −2 −1 0 1 2 3 4 5 6 7 8 9 10

We often use negative numbers in the context of temperature.

Example

The temperature is 6°C. It falls 8°C.

What is the new temperature?

Answer −2°C.

A

Copy and complete by writing the missing numbers in the boxes

1 −7 ☐ ☐ ☐ 1 3 5

5 6 4 ☐ ☐ ☐ −4 −6

2 10 7 4 1 ☐ ☐ ☐

6 ☐ ☐ ☐ −1 −3 −5 −7

3 −13 −10 −7 ☐ ☐ ☐ 5

7 9 6 3 0 ☐ ☐ ☐

4 −10 −6 ☐ ☐ ☐ 10 14

8 11 7 3 ☐ ☐ ☐ −13

Put these numbers in order, smallest first.

9   −8 0
     6   −5
      −3 4

10   −10 3
      1   −4
        8 −1

11   9 0
      −7   −2
        2 4

12   −6
     3   −3 1
      −1 5

Look at the scale.

13 What temperatures are shown by the letters?

14 Which letter shows the coldest temperature?

15 Give the difference in temperature between:
a) A and B   b) A and C   c) B and C.

16 What would the temperature be:
a) if it was at A and fell 13°C?
b) if it was at B and rose 19°C?
c) if it was at C and fell 15°C?

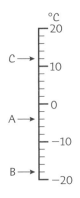

17 The temperature is −5°C and it rises by 10°C.
What is the new temperature?

18 The temperature is 3°C and it falls by 10°C.
What is the new temperature?

B

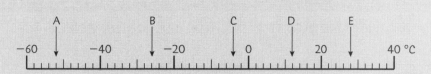

Scale: −60 ... A ... −40 ... B ... −20 ... C ... 0 ... D ... 20 ... E ... 40 °C

1. What temperatures are shown by the letters?
2. Give the difference in temperature between:
   a) C and D
   b) B and C
   c) C and E
   d) B and D.
3. What would the temperature be if it was:
   a) at A and rose 24°C?
   b) at D and fell 18°C?
   c) at C and fell 36°C?
   d) at B and rose 36°C?

Copy and complete the tables showing changes in temperature.

4

OLD	CHANGE	NEW
5°C	−9°C	−4°C
−3°C	+10°C	
−19°C	+13°C	
9°C	−15°C	
−12°C	+8°C	
13°C	−16°C	

5

OLD	CHANGE	NEW
−6°C	+8°C	2°C
	−6°C	−2°C
	+4°C	−13°C
	−8°C	−4°C
	+20°C	12°C
	−12°C	−17°C

6

OLD	CHANGE	NEW
9°C		−4°C
1°C		−11°C
4°C		−5°C
−5°C		9°C
−3°C		−16°C
6°C		−4°C

C

Copy and complete the table showing the average temperatures recorded in January and July at places in different countries.

1

Country	January	July	Range
U.S.A.	−7°C	26°C	33°C
Greenland	−35°C	−1°C	
Germany	−2°C	18°C	
Japan	−9°C	21°C	
Switzerland	−6°C	11°C	
Iran	−3°C		40°C
China	−19°C		42°C
Poland	−5°C		20°C
Norway	−14°C		23°C
Korea	−22°C		42°C
Romania		24°C	29°C
Russia		18°C	58°C
Canada		20°C	39°C
Sweden		16°C	20°C

Copy and complete this table showing the goal difference of the top and bottom six football teams in the 1999–2000 Premiership.

2

Team	Goals for	Goals against	Goal difference
Man. Utd	97	45	
Arsenal	73	43	
Leeds	58		+15
Liverpool	51		+21
Chelsea		34	+19
Aston Villa		35	+11
⋮	⋮	⋮	⋮
Southampton	45	62	
Derby	44	57	
Bradford	38		−30
Wimbledon	46		−28
Sheff. Wed.		70	−32
Watford		77	−42

On this page you will learn to extend number sequences.

To find the rule that links the numbers study the gaps.

Examples

4	0	−4	−8	−12	The rule is 'subtract 4.'
3	6	12	24	48	The rule is 'multiply by 2'.
1	3	6	10	15	The rule is 'add one more each time'.

A

Write the first six numbers in each sequence.

	Start at	Rule			Start at	Rule			Start at	Rule
1	210	−4		**6**	0·6	+0·1		**11**	0·01	+0·02
2	65	+4		**7**	201	+101		**12**	3·5	−0·5
3	62	+5		**8**	47	+9		**13**	76	−11
4	−60	+5		**9**	425	−50		**14**	1·25	+0·25
5	−1	−1		**10**	−3	−2		**15**	−18	−2

B

Complete these sequences by filling in the boxes. Write down the rule each time.

1 −4 −3 −2 −1 □ □ □
2 1·2 2·4 3·6 4·8 □ □ □
3 □ □ □ 64 70 76 82
4 □ □ □ 0·9 1·1 1·3 1·5
5 19 38 □ □ □ 114 133
6 0·09 0·18 □ □ □ 0·54 0·63
7 −33 −23 −13 −3 □ □ □
8 □ 42 63 □ 105 126 □

9 115 □ 101 □ 87 □ 73
10 100 □ 81 □ 66 □ 55
11 □ −5 □ □ 4 7 10
12 □ 4 □ □ 25 36 49
13 □ □ □ −5 −8 −11 −14
14 2 4 □ 16 □ 64 □
15 290 □ 170 □ □ 65 50
16 1·3 □ 2·1 □ □ 3·3 3·7

C

Copy these sequences and write the next three numbers. Write down the rule each time.

1 −8 −6 −4 −2
2 2·1 4·2 6·3 8·4
3 25 20 15 10
4 1·5 2·0 3·0 4·5
5 −15 −11 −7 −3
6 10·0 10·1 10·3 10·6

7 11 30 49 68
8 15 11 7 3
9 100 82 64 46
10 49 64 81 100
11 124 99 74 49
12 0·05 0·1 0·15 0·2

13 1·0 0·75 0·5 0·25
14 154 132 110 88
15 3·0 2·25 1·5 0·75
16 −21 −15 −10 −6
17 50 99 148 197
18 0·3 0·41 0·53 0·66

On this page you will learn to recognise multiples.

Multiples are the numbers in a multiplication table.

Example

The multiples of 3 are the numbers in the 3 times table.

3, 6, 9, 12, 15, 18 . . . 48, 51, 54, 57, 60 . . . 150, 153, 156, 159 and so on.

A

Write the first six multiples of each of these numbers.

1. 3
2. 7
3. 9
4. 25
5. 12
6. 20

Write Yes or No.

7. Is 48 a multiple of 6?
8. Is 54 a multiple of 7?
9. Is 120 a multiple of 8?
10. Is 74 a multiple of 9?
11. Is 77 a multiple of 11?
12. Is 180 a multiple of 18?

13. Is 80 a multiple of 12?
14. Is 300 a multiple of 15?
15. Is 450 a multiple of 50?
16. Is 93 a multiple of 6?
17. Is 81 a multiple of 9?
18. Is 155 a multiple of 25?

19. Is 98 a multiple of 11?
20. Is 140 a multiple of 20?
21. Is 63 a multiple of 7?
22. Is 31 a multiple of 13?
23. Is 60 a multiple of 12?
24. Is 98 a multiple of 8?

B

Which number should not be in the box?

1. Multiples of 8
120, 64, 36, 48

2. Multiples of 6
46, 24, 84, 54

3. Multiples of 7
84, 21, 56, 48

4. Multiples of 30
150, 90, 230, 60

5. Multiples of 11
110, 122, 99, 143

6. Multiples of 9
64, 108, 81, 45

Look at the numbers in the ring. Write down the numbers which are multiples of:

7. 4
8. 6
9. 9
10. 10

24 60 36 48 180
54 30 32 40 27

C

The lowest common multiple of two or more numbers is the smallest number that can be divided exactly by each of them.

Examples

The lowest common multiple of 2 and 5 is 10.
The lowest common multiple of 10 and 12 is 60.
The lowest common multiple of 2, 5 and 6 is 30.

Find the lowest common multiple of each of these pairs or groups of numbers.

1. 2 and 3
2. 3 and 4
3. 4 and 5
4. 3 and 5
5. 6 and 8
6. 4 and 10
7. 2 and 7
8. 10 and 6
9. 8 and 4
10. 4 and 6
11. 5 and 9
12. 10 and 8
13. 2, 5 and 10
14. 2, 7 and 21
15. 4, 10 and 25
16. 2, 3 and 4
17. 3, 4 and 5
18. 4, 8 and 12
19. 2, 3 and 5
20. 4, 5 and 6
21. 3, 4 and 10
22. 3, 4 and 6
23. 3, 4 and 9
24. 2, 5 and 7

On this page you will learn to use tests of divisibility.

Whole numbers are divisible by:
100	if the last 2 digits are 00.	10	if the last digit is 0.
2	if the last digit is even.	5	if the last digit is 0 or 5.
3	if the sum of the digits is divisible by 3.	4	if the last 2 digits are divisible by 4.
6	if the number is even and divisible by 3.	8	if the last 3 digits are divisible by 8.
9	if the sum of the digits is divisible by 9.	25	if the last 2 digits are 00, 25, 50 or 75.

 A

Decide if each number is divisible by the number in the box. Write Yes or No.

100		2		4		5		10
1 400	**5** 43	**9** 132	**13** 154	**17** 500
2 80	**6** 90	**10** 46	**14** 160	**18** 25
3 940	**7** 285	**11** 508	**15** 375	**19** 64
4 6000	**8** 178	**12** 222	**16** 82	**20** 230

B

Write True or False for each of the following statements.

1 353 is divisible by 3.   **6** 1056 is divisible by 8.   **11** 474 is divisible by 6.

2 48 is divisible by 4.   **7** 1763 is divisible by 9.   **12** 2148 is divisible by 8.

3 1458 is divisible by 9.   **8** 885 is divisible by 3.   **13** 875 is divisible by 25.

4 158 is divisible by 6.   **9** 2255 is divisible by 25.   **14** 182 is divisible by 4.

5 1900 is divisible by 25.   **10** 376 is divisible by 4.   **15** 798 is divisible by 3.

C

Copy and complete the table, using ticks and crosses to show divisibility.

NUMBER	DIVISIBLE BY							
	3	4	5	6	8	9	10	25
336	✓							
740	✗							
675								
2952								
825								
6210								
1336								
2700								

On this page you will learn to recognise prime numbers.

A prime number is a number which is divisible by only two different numbers: by itself and by one.

The first four prime numbers are 2, 3, 5 and 7. Notice that 1 is *not* a prime number. 4, 6, 8, 9 and 10 are not prime numbers because they are divisible by at least one of the first four prime numbers.

To find out if a two-digit number is a prime number you need to work out if it is divisible by one of the first four prime numbers, 2, 3, 5 and 7.

Examples

28 is divisible by 7.	28 is not a prime number.
29 is not divisible by 2, 3, 5 or 7.	29 is a prime number.
30 is divisible by 2, 3 and 5.	30 is not a prime number.
31 is not divisible by 2, 3, 5 or 7.	31 is a prime number.

A

Write down the prime number in each group.

1. 7, 8, 9
2. 16, 17, 18
3. 21, 22, 23
4. 30, 31, 32
5. 47, 48, 49
6. 57, 58, 59
7. 66, 67, 68
8. 73, 74, 75
9. Find all the prime numbers below 50. There are 15. (Remember, 1 is not a prime number.)
10. Find the next prime number after 37.

B

Write down the two numbers in each group which are *not* prime numbers.

1. 1   11   21   31
2. 40   41   42   43
3. 33   43   53   63
4. 47   57   67   77
5. 51   61   71   81
6. 67   77   87   97

Write down the next prime number after:

7. 30
8. 45
9. 50
10. 75
11. Find all the prime numbers below 100. There are 25.

C

In the questions in this section you may need to work out if a number is divisible by prime numbers other than 2, 3, 5 and 7. 121 is not a prime number because it is divisible by 11.

Example

Which of these are prime numbers?

1. 103
2. 111
3. 116
4. 127
5. 133
6. 139
7. 153
8. 181

Explain why the following are not prime numbers.

9. 74
10. 87
11. 91
12. 115
13. 143
14. 169
15. 187
16. 289

On this page you will learn to identify prime factors and use them for finding products.

Factors are numbers that divide exactly into another number.
It is useful to think of factors as pairs of numbers whose product is the target number.

Example

Find the factors of 12.　　1×12　2×6　3×4　　Factors of 12: 1, 2, 3, 4, 6, 12.

A factor which is also a prime number is a *prime factor*.

To find the prime factors of a number we can use a factor tree.

A factor tree for 63
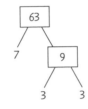
$63 = 7 \times 3 \times 3$

A factor tree for 36
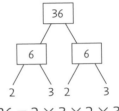
$36 = 2 \times 3 \times 2 \times 3$

Prime factors can be used to find products.

Example

$42 \times 36 = 42 \times 2 \times 3 \times 2 \times 3 = 126 \times 2 \times 2 \times 3 = 252 \times 2 \times 3 = 756 \times 2 = 1512$

A

Find all the factors of the following numbers.

1　6
2　16
3　20
4　22
5　27
6　30
7　32
8　36

Copy and complete as in the example above.

9　$13 \times 6 = 13 \times 3 \times 2 = \square$
10　$16 \times 12 = 16 \times 3 \times 2 \times 2 = \square$
11　$24 \times 8 = 24 \times 2 \times 2 \times 2 = \square$
12　$31 \times 14 = 31 \times 7 \times 2 = \square$
13　$23 \times 15 = 23 \times 5 \times 3 = \square$
14　$25 \times 18 = 25 \times 2 \times 3 \times 3 = \square$
15　$35 \times 9 = 35 \times 3 \times 3 = \square$

B

Use a factor tree to find all the prime factors of:

1　24
2　40
3　42
4　54
5　72
6　75
7　88
8　90

Break the second number down into prime factors to help work out:

9　31×12
10　14×25
11　32×20
12　38×24
13　39×36
14　51×42.

C

Use a factor tree to find all the prime factors of:

1　48
2　60
3　81
4　84
5　100
6　144
7　162
8　256.

Break the second number down into prime factors to help work out:

9　61×48
10　53×42
11　56×45
12　65×56
13　76×64
14　89×72.

On this page you will learn to recognise square numbers.

When a number is multiplied by itself you get a square number.
They are called square numbers because they make square patterns.

$1^2 = 1 \times 1 = 1$ $2^2 = 2 \times 2 = 4$ $3^2 = 3 \times 3 = 9$ $4^2 = 4 \times 4 = 16$

A

1 Complete this table up to 12^2.

$1^2 = 1 \times 1 = 1$

$2^2 = 2 \times 2 = 4$

$3^2 = 3 \times 3 = 9$

Work out

2 $4^2 + 2^2$

8 $10^2 + 7^2$

3 $5^2 + 3^2$

9 $9^2 + 1^2$

4 $6^2 + 1^2$

10 $8^2 + 5^2$

5 $5^2 - 3^2$

11 $9^2 - 4^2$

6 $8^2 - 6^2$

12 $10^2 - 6^2$

7 $6^2 - 3^2$

13 $8^2 - 7^2$

14 Here is a 5×5 square divided into eight smaller squares.

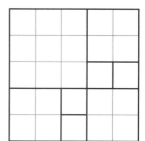

Draw a 7×7 square and design a pattern which divides it into nine smaller squares.

B

Work out

1 20^2 **5** 31^2

2 21^2 **6** 13^2

3 19^2 **7** 40^2

4 15^2 **8** 100^2

Use a calculator to find out which number, when multiplied by itself, gives a product of:

9 729   **13** 2116

10 196   **14** 784

11 1225   **15** 1024

12 484   **16** 6889.

Find a pair of square numbers which give a total of:

17 13   **21** 73

18 40   **22** 181

19 125   **23** 97

20 74   **24** 113.

Find a pair of square numbers which give a difference of:

25 7   **29** 80

26 84   **30** 300

27 45   **31** 32

28 39   **32** 105.

C

Lagrange's Theorem
A famous mathematician called Lagrange proved that every whole number could be written as the sum of four or fewer square numbers.

Examples

$19 = 16 + 1 + 1 + 1$

$35 = 25 + 9 + 1$

$47 = 36 + 9 + 1 + 1$

Make the following numbers from four or fewer square numbers.

1 10   **9** 96

2 15   **10** 120

3 24   **11** 141

4 48   **12** 160

5 57   **13** 199

6 62   **14** 230

7 72   **15** 358

8 80   **16** 423

17 A square playground has a perimeter of 100 metres. What is its area?

On these pages you will learn to change a fraction to an equivalent fraction by cancelling or by multiplying.

Equivalent fractions are fractions that look different but are the same.

Example

 $\dfrac{2}{5} = \dfrac{8}{20}$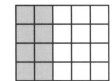

A fraction can be changed to an equivalent fraction by:

CANCELLING

Example $\dfrac{6}{9} \dfrac{(\div 3)}{(\div 3)} = \dfrac{2}{3}$

MULTIPLYING

Example $\dfrac{3}{4} \dfrac{(\times 4)}{(\times 4)} = \dfrac{12}{16}$

A

Write the equivalent fractions shown by the shaded areas in each pair of diagrams.

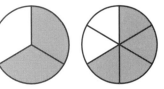

B

Copy and complete these equivalent fractions.

1. $\dfrac{2}{3} = \dfrac{\square}{12}$ 4. $\dfrac{2}{15} = \dfrac{\square}{30}$ 7. $\dfrac{3}{8} = \dfrac{9}{\square}$ 10. $\dfrac{7}{8} = \dfrac{35}{\square}$ 13. $\dfrac{4}{9} = \dfrac{\square}{36}$

2. $\dfrac{3}{10} = \dfrac{\square}{100}$ 5. $\dfrac{3}{5} = \dfrac{\square}{20}$ 8. $\dfrac{5}{7} = \dfrac{25}{\square}$ 11. $\dfrac{3}{4} = \dfrac{\square}{28}$ 14. $\dfrac{7}{20} = \dfrac{\square}{100}$

3. $\dfrac{1}{4} = \dfrac{\square}{16}$ 6. $\dfrac{1}{6} = \dfrac{4}{\square}$ 9. $\dfrac{2}{3} = \dfrac{12}{\square}$ 12. $\dfrac{2}{5} = \dfrac{\square}{25}$ 15. $\dfrac{2}{7} = \dfrac{\square}{21}$

Cancel each fraction into its simplest form.

16. $\dfrac{5}{20}$ 18. $\dfrac{8}{40}$ 20. $\dfrac{90}{100}$ 22. $\dfrac{14}{16}$ 24. $\dfrac{16}{28}$ 26. $\dfrac{9}{12}$ 28. $\dfrac{8}{12}$ 30. $\dfrac{25}{80}$

17. $\dfrac{6}{14}$ 19. $\dfrac{15}{27}$ 21. $\dfrac{10}{15}$ 23. $\dfrac{36}{60}$ 25. $\dfrac{28}{35}$ 27. $\dfrac{48}{100}$ 29. $\dfrac{30}{36}$ 31. $\dfrac{20}{32}$

Continue these fraction chains for five further terms.

32. $\dfrac{1}{3} = \dfrac{2}{6} = \dfrac{3}{9}$ 33. $\dfrac{3}{4} = \dfrac{6}{8} = \dfrac{9}{12}$ 34. $\dfrac{7}{10} = \dfrac{14}{20} = \dfrac{21}{30}$

C

Pick out the letters above the fractions equivalent to the fraction in the brackets.
Rearrange those letters to make a word using the clue.

1. $\left(\dfrac{1}{10},\ \text{a food}\right)$

E	C	N	R	L	A	B	E	D	T
$\dfrac{3}{30}$	$\dfrac{6}{66}$	$\dfrac{2}{10}$	$\dfrac{8}{80}$	$\dfrac{20}{100}$	$\dfrac{2}{20}$	$\dfrac{4}{40}$	$\dfrac{5}{25}$	$\dfrac{9}{90}$	$\dfrac{10}{50}$

5. $\left(\dfrac{1}{4},\ \text{a city in England}\right)$

C	H	E	R	S	D	T	L	A	E
$\dfrac{4}{12}$	$\dfrac{7}{30}$	$\dfrac{2}{8}$	$\dfrac{8}{24}$	$\dfrac{5}{20}$	$\dfrac{3}{12}$	$\dfrac{10}{44}$	$\dfrac{6}{24}$	$\dfrac{15}{40}$	$\dfrac{4}{16}$

2. $\left(\dfrac{1}{2},\ \text{a fruit}\right)$

A	P	G	L	E	N	H	P	C	R
$\dfrac{7}{14}$	$\dfrac{6}{16}$	$\dfrac{8}{16}$	$\dfrac{4}{10}$	$\dfrac{2}{4}$	$\dfrac{3}{9}$	$\dfrac{12}{20}$	$\dfrac{5}{10}$	$\dfrac{25}{40}$	$\dfrac{9}{18}$

6. $\left(\dfrac{3}{8},\ \text{a tool}\right)$

H	D	I	E	P	L	A	S	T	C
$\dfrac{15}{40}$	$\dfrac{14}{32}$	$\dfrac{21}{56}$	$\dfrac{6}{16}$	$\dfrac{8}{20}$	$\dfrac{24}{64}$	$\dfrac{36}{80}$	$\dfrac{9}{24}$	$\dfrac{20}{48}$	$\dfrac{27}{72}$

3. $\left(\dfrac{2}{3},\ \text{a European country}\right)$

A	N	G	E	T	S	L	E	D	W
$\dfrac{6}{10}$	$\dfrac{8}{12}$	$\dfrac{21}{30}$	$\dfrac{4}{6}$	$\dfrac{8}{15}$	$\dfrac{18}{27}$	$\dfrac{15}{24}$	$\dfrac{10}{15}$	$\dfrac{20}{30}$	$\dfrac{6}{9}$

7. $\left(\dfrac{3}{5},\ \text{an English county}\right)$

N	O	D	R	E	N	F	V	L	K
$\dfrac{9}{16}$	$\dfrac{12}{20}$	$\dfrac{27}{45}$	$\dfrac{20}{30}$	$\dfrac{6}{10}$	$\dfrac{15}{25}$	$\dfrac{33}{50}$	$\dfrac{9}{15}$	$\dfrac{20}{35}$	$\dfrac{30}{55}$

4. $\left(\dfrac{3}{4},\ \text{a boy's name}\right)$

O	N	C	E	I	R	L	A	N	Y
$\dfrac{4}{6}$	$\dfrac{6}{8}$	$\dfrac{16}{20}$	$\dfrac{75}{100}$	$\dfrac{9}{15}$	$\dfrac{10}{16}$	$\dfrac{30}{40}$	$\dfrac{24}{30}$	$\dfrac{9}{12}$	$\dfrac{15}{20}$

8. $\left(\dfrac{5}{6},\ \text{a girl's name}\right)$

A	P	A	L	T	I	R	N	O	D
$\dfrac{25}{30}$	$\dfrac{55}{60}$	$\dfrac{20}{26}$	$\dfrac{10}{12}$	$\dfrac{15}{24}$	$\dfrac{40}{48}$	$\dfrac{30}{42}$	$\dfrac{50}{60}$	$\dfrac{45}{36}$	$\dfrac{15}{18}$

9. Now make up a similar problem of your own.

On this page you will use your knowledge of equivalent fractions to compare and order fractions.

Example

Arrange $\frac{1}{2}, \frac{3}{5}, \frac{8}{20}$ in ascending order.

Convert the fractions to a common denominator. $\frac{1}{2} = \frac{5}{10}, \quad \frac{3}{5} = \frac{6}{10}, \quad \frac{8}{20} = \frac{4}{10}$

Arrange in ascending order. $\frac{8}{20}, \frac{1}{2}, \frac{3}{5}$.

A

Which of the fractions in the box are:

1 equal to one half?

2 less than one half?

3 greater than one half?

$\frac{1}{6}$	$\frac{6}{10}$	$\frac{3}{8}$	$\frac{50}{100}$
$\frac{3}{5}$	$\frac{7}{16}$	$\frac{11}{20}$	$\frac{6}{12}$

4 Match the fractions to the letters.

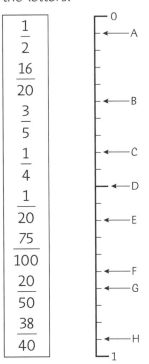

B

Arrange in ascending order.

1 $\frac{1}{2}, \quad \frac{2}{3}, \quad \frac{4}{12}, \quad \frac{5}{6}$

2 $\frac{5}{16}, \quad \frac{3}{8}, \quad \frac{1}{4}, \quad \frac{1}{2}$

3 $\frac{5}{9}, \quad \frac{3}{4}, \quad \frac{2}{3}, \quad \frac{1}{2}, \quad \frac{5}{6}$

4 $1\frac{3}{4}, \quad 2\frac{1}{4}, \quad 1\frac{3}{10}, \quad 1\frac{1}{2}$

5 $2\frac{2}{3}, \quad 1\frac{3}{8}, \quad 2\frac{1}{2}, \quad 1\frac{3}{4}$

6 $1\frac{3}{5}, \quad 2\frac{7}{20}, \quad 1\frac{7}{10}, \quad 2\frac{33}{100}$

7 Match the fractions to the letters.

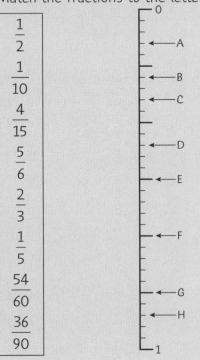

C

Find the number which is half way between each pair of numbers.

1 1 and $1\frac{1}{2}$

2 $\frac{3}{10}$ and $\frac{1}{2}$

3 $\frac{1}{2}$ and $\frac{3}{4}$

4 $\frac{4}{9}$ and $\frac{2}{3}$

5 $1\frac{1}{4}$ and $1\frac{5}{12}$

6 $1\frac{1}{4}$ and $1\frac{1}{2}$

7 $2\frac{1}{3}$ and $2\frac{2}{3}$

8 $2\frac{1}{5}$ and $2\frac{2}{5}$

9 $\frac{1}{2}$ and $\frac{1}{3}$

10 $\frac{5}{8}$ and $\frac{3}{4}$

11 $1\frac{2}{5}$ and $1\frac{1}{2}$

12 $1\frac{2}{3}$ and $1\frac{5}{6}$

13 $4\frac{3}{5}$ and $4\frac{7}{10}$

14 $2\frac{1}{3}$ and $2\frac{1}{4}$

15 $1\frac{3}{4}$ and $1\frac{3}{5}$

16 $\frac{2}{3}$ and $\frac{3}{5}$

17 $\frac{4}{7}$ and $\frac{1}{2}$

18 $\frac{7}{9}$ and $\frac{3}{4}$

19 $2\frac{3}{8}$ and $2\frac{1}{3}$

20 $1\frac{5}{6}$ and $2\frac{3}{4}$

On this page you will learn to change an improper fraction to a mixed number and vice versa.

Examples

1. Change $\frac{19}{5}$ to a mixed number.

   Divide numerator by denominator. $\quad \frac{19}{5} = 19 \div 5 = 3$ rem. 4

   Put remainder over denominator. $\qquad = 3\frac{4}{5}$

2. Change $7\frac{2}{7}$ to an improper fraction.

   Multiply whole number by denominator. $\quad 7 \times 7 = 49$

   Add the numerator. $\qquad\qquad\qquad 49 + 2 = 51$

   Put sum over denominator. $\qquad\qquad 7\frac{2}{7} = \frac{51}{7}$

A

Write the shaded areas as both mixed numbers and improper fractions.

1

2

3

4

5

6

7

8

9

10

B

Copy and complete.

1. $\dfrac{11}{3} = 3\dfrac{\square}{3}$

2. $\dfrac{21}{4} = 5\dfrac{\square}{4}$

3. $\dfrac{23}{6} = \square\dfrac{5}{6}$

4. $\dfrac{17}{7} = \square\dfrac{3}{7}$

5. $\dfrac{28}{5} = \square\dfrac{\square}{\square}$

6. $\dfrac{48}{10} = \square\dfrac{\square}{\square}$

7. $\dfrac{41}{12} = \square\dfrac{\square}{\square}$

8. $\dfrac{123}{50} = \square\dfrac{\square}{\square}$

9. $4\dfrac{1}{3} = \dfrac{13}{\square}$

10. $7\dfrac{3}{5} = \dfrac{38}{\square}$

11. $4\dfrac{4}{7} = \dfrac{\square}{7}$

12. $2\dfrac{5}{9} = \dfrac{\square}{9}$

13. $3\dfrac{7}{8} = \dfrac{\square}{\square}$

14. $2\dfrac{71}{100} = \dfrac{\square}{\square}$

C

Change to mixed numbers.

1. $\frac{17}{3}$ 7. $\frac{77}{10}$

2. $\frac{29}{4}$ 8. $\frac{55}{12}$

3. $\frac{35}{6}$ 9. $\frac{63}{20}$

4. $\frac{20}{7}$ 10. $\frac{119}{25}$

5. $\frac{31}{8}$ 11. $\frac{163}{50}$

6. $\frac{43}{9}$ 12. $\frac{453}{100}$

Change to improper fractions.

13. $5\frac{2}{3}$ 19. $5\frac{2}{9}$

14. $8\frac{3}{4}$ 20. $9\frac{7}{10}$

15. $6\frac{3}{5}$ 21. $3\frac{5}{12}$

16. $5\frac{1}{6}$ 22. $4\frac{19}{20}$

17. $6\frac{3}{7}$ 23. $6\frac{10}{11}$

18. $7\frac{5}{8}$ 24. $12\frac{24}{25}$

Answer True or False.

25. $\frac{19}{4} = 4\frac{3}{4}$

26. $\frac{67}{5} < \frac{124}{10}$

27. $6\frac{1}{2} > \frac{45}{7}$

28. $\frac{76}{9} = 8\frac{2}{3}$

29. $\frac{34}{5} < \frac{40}{6}$

30. $\frac{111}{8} > 14\frac{1}{4}$

On these pages you will learn what each digit in a decimal fraction represents.

Examples

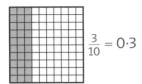

$$\frac{3}{10} = 0.3$$

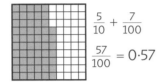

$$\frac{5}{10} + \frac{7}{100}$$

$$\frac{57}{100} = 0.57$$

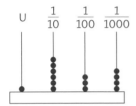

$$1 + \frac{6}{10} + \frac{3}{100} + \frac{4}{1000}$$

$$1\frac{634}{1000} = 1.634$$

The value of a digit depends upon its position in a number.

Each digit is 10 times higher than the digit to the right. This applies to decimal fractions as well as to whole numbers.

T	U	.	$\frac{1}{10}$	$\frac{1}{100}$	$\frac{1}{1000}$
$70 =$ 7	0	.	0		
$7 =$	7	.	0		
$\frac{7}{10} =$	0	.	7		
$\frac{7}{100} =$	0	.	0	7	
$\frac{7}{1000} =$	0	.	0	0	7

A

Express the shaded part of each diagram as a fraction and as a decimal fraction.

1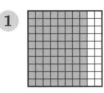

3

2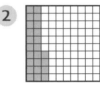

4

Write each number shown by the arrows as a decimal fraction.

5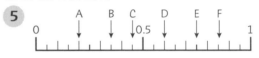

6

Give the value of the underlined figure in each of these numbers.

7 16.<u>8</u>   11 0.0<u>6</u>   15 2.0<u>3</u>

8 9.5<u>2</u>   12 3.<u>2</u>9   16 9.<u>1</u>7

9 24.<u>7</u>6   13 58.3<u>6</u>   17 0.83<u>1</u>

10 1<u>5</u>.43   14 8.<u>5</u>   18 12.<u>6</u>2

Give the next five terms in each of these sequences.

19 0.01, 0.03, 0.05, 0.07, 0.09

20 1.01, 1.02, 1.03, 1.04, 1.05

21 0.9, 0.92, 0.94, 0.96, 0.98

22 1.6, 1.65, 1.7, 1.75, 1.8

B

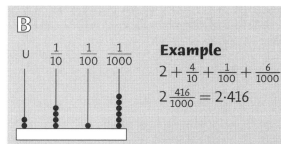

Example

$2 + \frac{4}{10} + \frac{1}{100} + \frac{6}{1000}$

$2\frac{416}{1000} = 2 \cdot 416$

Write the decimal fraction shown on each abacus.

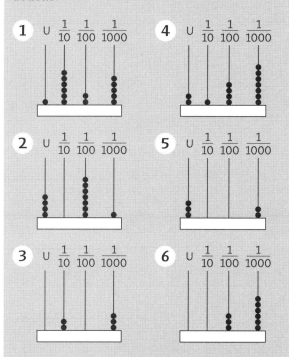

Write these numbers as decimal fractions.

7 $\frac{1}{100}$ 11 $9\frac{7}{100}$ 15 $8\frac{254}{1000}$

8 $2\frac{76}{100}$ 12 $\frac{43}{1000}$ 16 $72\frac{4}{100}$

9 $\frac{397}{1000}$ 13 $\frac{6}{1000}$ 17 $5\frac{3}{1000}$

10 $4\frac{821}{1000}$ 14 $3\frac{74}{1000}$ 18 $26\frac{26}{1000}$

Give the value of the underlined figure in each of these numbers.

19 6·3<u>4</u>   23 <u>1</u>8·196   27 <u>3</u>6·078

20 12·8<u>5</u>   24 1·0<u>3</u>5   28 4·3<u>4</u>

21 6·42<u>7</u>   25 0·<u>7</u>08   29 4·2<u>2</u>2

22 <u>1</u>5·8   26 15·<u>9</u>2   30 0·5<u>1</u>6

C

Write each number shown by the arrows as a decimal fraction.

1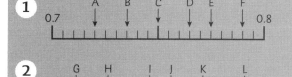

2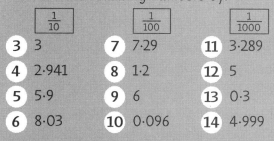

Increase the following numbers by:

$\frac{1}{10}$	$\frac{1}{100}$	$\frac{1}{1000}$

3 3   7 7·29   11 3·289

4 2·941   8 1·2   12 5

5 5·9   9 6   13 0·3

6 8·03   10 0·096   14 4·999

Give the next five terms in each of these sequences.

15 0·592, 0·593, 0·594, 0·595, 0·596

16 0·06, 0·065, 0·07, 0·075, 0·08

17 2·99, 2·992, 2·994, 2·996, 2·998

18 1·02, 1·016, 1·012, 1·008, 1·004

Copy and complete.

19 $1·683 + 0·05 = \square$

20 $5·134 - 0·009 = \square$

21 $2·791 + 0·8 = \square$

22 $1·482 - 0·6 = \square$

23 $3·164 + 0·07 = \square$

24 $3·261 - 0·08 = \square$

25 $0·72 + \square = 0·743$

26 $1·298 - \square = 0·898$

27 $3·592 + \square = 3·612$

28 $2·793 - \square = 2·788$

29 $0·063 + \square = 0·123$

30 $9·487 - \square = 9·478$

On this page you will learn to order a set of decimals.

Write the set of decimals in a line with the decimal points in a column.

Fill in any empty spaces with zeros. This makes it easier to compare the decimals.

Example

Write 1·41, 1·4, 1·141, 1 in ascending order.

Write in column.	Put in zeros.	Arrange in order.
1·41	1·410	1
1·4	1·400	1·141
1·141	1·141	1·4
1	1·000	1·41

 A

Copy and complete by writing < or > in the box.

1 5·88 ☐ 8·5

2 4·2 ☐ 4·9

3 6·7 ☐ 6·37

4 3·46 ☐ 4·36

5 2·71 ☐ 1·72

6 9·58 ☐ 9·8

7 8·37 ☐ 8·73

8 5·31 ☐ 5·13

9 Copy the line and locate the numbers.

    | 2·0 2·03 2·05 1·95 1·97 2·07 |

    1.9   2.1

B

Arrange these decimals in ascending order.

1 6·29, 0·69, 0·609, 6·09

2 5·227, 2·257, 5·27, 2·57

3 9·123, 9·23, 0·923, 92·3

4 8·77, 8·272, 2·788, 2·87

5 Copy the line and locate the numbers.

    | 1·98   1·935 1·99 |
    | 1·965 1·915 1·95 |

    1.9   2.0

C

Arrange these decimals in ascending order.

1 5·656, 55·65, 5·56, 5·556, 5·66

2 4·944, 4·99, 4·9, 4·499, 4·494

3 0·781, 1·7, 0·187, 0·178, 0·71

4 2·303, 0·322, 2·033, 2·32, 0·33

5 2·222, 2·2, 22·22, 22·2, 2·22

6 1·414, 1·144, 14·14, 1·114, 1·44

7 6·606, 6·66, 6·066, 60·6, 6·06

8 1·771, 1·717, 1·177, 1·17, 1·7

9 Draw a line from 0·99 to 1·01 with 20 divisions. Show these numbers on your line.

    | 1·00 0·995 1·002 1·006 0·992 1·008 |

On this page you will learn to round decimals to the nearest number or tenth.

To round a decimal fraction to the nearest whole number look at the tenths column.
To round a decimal fraction to the nearest tenth look at the hundredths column.
If the number in that column is less than 5, round down.
If the number in that column is greater than 5, round up.

Examples

To the nearest whole number,   3·5 rounds to 4   5·49 rounds to 5
To the nearest tenth,   2·61 rounds to 2·6   4·372 rounds to 4·4.

A

Round to the nearest whole number.

1	10·4	**7**	17·6
2	1·7	**8**	9·47
3	7·5	**9**	12·3
4	4·23	**10**	11·51
5	8·25	**11**	14·28
6	0·83	**12**	3·61

Round to the nearest pound.

13	£6·70	**19**	£2·09
14	£2·40	**20**	£1·37
15	£5·50	**21**	£0·85
16	£12·26	**22**	£3·44
17	£4·91	**23**	£11·52
18	£10·73	**24**	£8·65

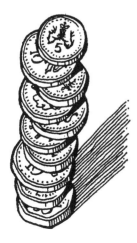

B

Round to the nearest:

1		0.1	
1	16·48	**6**	1·249
2	8·943	**7**	10·66
3	17·37	**8**	0·152
4	4·539	**9**	2·58
5	13·75	**10**	5·873

£1		10p	
11	£2·67	**16**	£5·73
12	£0·26	**17**	£0·26
13	£7·53	**18**	£8·05
14	£3·85	**19**	£16·34
15	£1·04	**20**	£4·98

1 m		10 cm	
21	8·60 m	**26**	9·04 m
22	2·28 m	**27**	1·46 m
23	5·47 m	**28**	4·55 m
24	0·93 m	**29**	8·63 m
25	7·52 m	**30**	2·97 m

C

1 Copy the table rounding the kilograms to the nearest 100 g.

Pounds	Kilograms
1	0·454
2	0·907
3	1·361
4	1·814
5	2·268
6	2·722
7	3·175
8	3·629
9	4·082

2 Copy the table rounding the litres to the nearest 100 ml.

Gallons	Litres
1	4·546
2	9·092
3	13·638
4	18·184
5	22·730
6	27·276
7	31·822
8	36·368
9	40·914

On this page you will learn to recognise equivalent fractions and decimals.

It is important to remember that:

$\frac{1}{10} = 0.1$ $\frac{2}{10} = 0.2$ $\frac{3}{10} = 0.3$ and so on.

$\frac{1}{100} = 0.01$ $\frac{2}{100} = 0.02$ $\frac{3}{100} = 0.03$ and so on.

$\frac{1}{1000} = 0.001$ $\frac{2}{1000} = 0.002$ $\frac{3}{1000} = 0.003$ and so on.

$\frac{1}{2} = 0.5$ $\frac{1}{4} = 0.25$ $\frac{3}{4} = 0.75$

A

Write True or False for each of the following statements.

1. $\frac{82}{100} = 0.08$
2. $\frac{7}{10} = 0.07$
3. $\frac{1}{4} = 0.25$
4. $\frac{1}{100} = 0.01$
5. $\frac{3}{4} = 0.34$
6. $\frac{1}{10} = 0.1$
7. $\frac{94}{100} = 0.94$
8. $\frac{1}{2} = 0.2$
9. $0.001 = \frac{1}{1000}$
10. $0.003 = \frac{3}{100}$
11. $0.2 = \frac{1}{2}$
12. $0.09 = \frac{9}{100}$
13. $0.521 = \frac{521}{1000}$
14. $0.23 = \frac{23}{1000}$
15. $0.75 = \frac{3}{4}$
16. $0.6 = \frac{6}{10}$

17. Match each of these fractions with one of these decimals.

$\frac{2}{10}$	0.5
$\frac{5}{100}$	0.75
$\frac{1}{2}$	0.05
$\frac{3}{10}$	0.3
$\frac{3}{4}$	0.55
$\frac{55}{100}$	0.2

B

Write as fractions.

1. 2.72
2. 0.692
3. 7.75
4. 3.427
5. 1.05
6. 6.081
7. 3.9
8. 5.006

Write as decimals.

9. £2$\frac{63}{100}$
10. £5$\frac{9}{10}$
11. £7$\frac{1}{4}$
12. £9$\frac{7}{100}$
13. 4$\frac{129}{1000}$ km
14. 2$\frac{3}{4}$ km
15. 6$\frac{3}{10}$ cm
16. 1$\frac{38}{1000}$ km

Give the answer as a decimal.

17. $0.38 + \frac{1}{4}$
18. $\frac{1}{2} - 0.24$
19. $\frac{3}{5} + 0.2$
20. $0.73 - \frac{4}{10}$
21. $0.6 + \frac{23}{100}$
22. $\frac{3}{4} - 0.6$

23. Write a decimal in the box. '2$\frac{3}{5}$ kg of sugar is ▢ kg.'

C

Write as fractions.

1. 8.54
2. 3.692
3. 6.06
4. 0.7
5. 11.025
6. 1.25
7. 9.001
8. 15.85
9. 4.247
10. 7.02
11. 2.031
12. 19.006

Write as decimals.

13. $\frac{75}{1000}$
14. $2\frac{4}{1000}$
15. $3\frac{19}{50}$
16. $2\frac{17}{20}$
17. £$\frac{17}{100}$
18. £9$\frac{11}{25}$
19. £1$\frac{12}{20}$
20. £3$\frac{2}{5}$
21. $2\frac{7}{20}$ m
22. $1\frac{4}{5}$ cm
23. $\frac{16}{25}$ m
24. $5\frac{49}{50}$ km

Write in ascending order.

25. $\frac{1}{4}$, 0.144, 0.41
26. 0.85, $\frac{4}{5}$, $\frac{5}{8}$
27. $\frac{7}{20}$, $\frac{207}{1000}$, 0.27
28. 0.408, $\frac{48}{100}$, 0.084
29. $\frac{499}{1000}$, 0.49, $\frac{4}{9}$
30. 0.503, $\frac{3}{5}$, 0.53

31. A full box of cereal contains $\frac{17}{40}$ kg. At breakfast 0.15 kg is used. How much cereal is left in the box?

On this page you will learn to find a fraction of a number or quantity.

Examples $\frac{1}{7}$ of $420 = 420 \div 7$ $\frac{5}{8}$ of $640 = (640 \div 8) \times 5$
                         $= 60$ $= 80 \times 5$
                                                                $= 400$

To find what fraction one quantity is of another, make a fraction by putting one quantity over the other.
TAKE CARE! The units of the two quantities must be the same.

Examples

What fraction of £2 is 35p?
Answer $= \frac{35}{200} = \frac{7}{40}$, because £2 = 200p.

What fraction of one metre is 25 cm?
Answer $= \frac{25}{100} = \frac{1}{4}$, because 1 m = 100 cm.

What fraction of one litre is 200 ml?
Answer $= \frac{200}{1000} = \frac{1}{5}$, because 1 litre = 1000 ml.

A

Find $\frac{1}{10}$ of:

1 700	**4** 5 m
2 280	**5** £2
3 1 m	**6** £3

Find $\frac{7}{10}$ of:

7 40	**10** 1 m
8 20	**11** £1
9 60 cm	**12** £5

Find $\frac{1}{8}$ of:

13 32	**16** 56 m
14 72	**17** 40p
15 24 cm	**18** 64p

Find $\frac{3}{4}$ of:

19 32	**22** 36 cm
20 24	**23** £1
21 1 m	**24** 60p

B

Find

1 $\frac{3}{5}$ of 40	**7** $\frac{63}{1000}$ of 1 kg
2 $\frac{5}{9}$ of 270	**8** $\frac{3}{10}$ of 3 kg
3 $\frac{9}{10}$ of 600	**9** $\frac{5}{6}$ of 480 g
4 $\frac{7}{10}$ of 5 m	**10** $\frac{4}{5}$ of 1 l
5 $\frac{29}{100}$ of 2 m	**11** $\frac{6}{7}$ of 42 l
6 $\frac{9}{1000}$ of 1 m	**12** $\frac{19}{100}$ of 3 l

What fraction of £1 is:

13 20p	**15** 75p
14 5p	**16** 4p?

What fraction of 1 litre is:

17 79 ml	**19** 250 ml
18 310 ml	**20** 10 ml?

What fraction of 1 metre is:

21 5 cm	**23** 60 cm
22 12 cm	**24** 35 cm?

C

Find

1 $\frac{7}{8}$ of 200	**7** $\frac{3}{5}$ of 6 kg
2 $\frac{4}{5}$ of 120	**8** $\frac{57}{100}$ of 4 kg
3 $\frac{7}{9}$ of 3600	**9** $\frac{7}{10}$ of 4 kg
4 $\frac{3}{10}$ of 4·2 m	**10** $\frac{12}{100}$ of 5 l
5 $\frac{19}{20}$ of 4 m	**11** $\frac{4}{50}$ of 2 l
6 $\frac{11}{1000}$ of 7 m	**12** $\frac{19}{1000}$ of 5 l

What fraction of £1 is:

13 17p	**15** £0·15
14 65p	**16** £0·02?

What fraction of 1 litre is:

17 5 ml	**19** 220 ml
18 125 ml	**20** 1 ml?

What fraction of 1 metre is:

21 2 cm	**23** 75 cm
22 2 mm	**24** 1 mm?

On these pages you will learn:

- **to understand percentage as the number of parts in 100.**

Per cent means out of 100.
Percentages are fractions with a
denominator of 100.
The symbol used for per cent is %.

23 small squares are shaded.
The fraction shaded $= \frac{23}{100}$.
The percentage
shaded $= 23\%$.

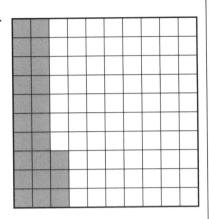

- **to recognise when percentages, decimals and fractions are equal.**

To express fractions as percentages, change them to
equivalent fractions with denominators of 100.

Examples

$\frac{3}{10} = \frac{30}{100} = 30\%$ $\frac{1}{2} = \frac{50}{100} = 50\%$

To express decimals as percentages, multiply by 100.

Examples

$0.53 = 53\%$ $0.2 = 20\%$

You need to know that:

$1 = \frac{100}{100} = 1.0 = 100\%$

$\frac{1}{10} = \frac{10}{100} = 0.1 = 10\%$

$\frac{1}{5} = \frac{20}{100} = 0.2 = 20\%$

$\frac{1}{100} = \frac{1}{100} = 0.01 = 1\%$

$\frac{1}{4} = \frac{25}{100} = 0.25 = 25\%$

$\frac{1}{2} = \frac{50}{100} = 0.5 = 50\%$

$\frac{3}{4} = \frac{75}{100} = 0.75 = 75\%$

A

Express each shaded area as:
a) a fraction   b) a decimal   c) a percentage.

9 What percentage of the 20 boxes contain:
   a) ticks   b) crosses   c) circles?

10 What percentage of the 20 boxes are blank?

✓		✗		✓
✓	✗	✓	✗	✓
✓	○	✓	○	✓
✓	✗	○	✗	✓

B

1 Copy and complete the table.

Fractions	$\frac{3}{10}$								$\frac{3}{100}$	$\frac{11}{50}$	$\frac{7}{20}$	$\frac{3}{25}$
Decimals	0·3				0·04	0·6	0·5	0·83				
Percentages	30%	26%	25%	70%								

What percentage could be used in each of these sentences?

2 Fay scored 38 out of 50 in her History Test.

3 Two fifths of the children in the class have fair hair.

4 Seven in every ten voters supported the winning candidate.

5 Half the chocolates in the box have hard centres.

6 The football team won 12 out of the 25 matches played.

7 Two in every hundred mothers gave birth to twins.

8 Michael Owen was on target with 4 out of his 5 shots at goal.

9 Three quarters of the audience were women.

10 It rained on eleven days in every twenty.

C

Write each fraction as:
a) a decimal
b) a percentage

Write each percentage as:
a) a fraction in its simplest form
b) a decimal.

1 $\frac{9}{10}$ 3 $\frac{3}{5}$ 5 $\frac{7}{25}$ 7 $\frac{9}{20}$ 9 62% 11 15% 13 64% 15 12·5%

2 $\frac{23}{50}$ 4 $\frac{78}{100}$ 6 $\frac{198}{200}$ 8 $\frac{470}{1000}$ 10 30% 12 43% 14 60% 16 2·5%

17 The girls' football team had a penalty competition. Copy and complete the table.

Name	Penalties	Goals	Scored (%)	Missed (%)
Leslie	25	16		
Kirsty	24	15		
Megan	20	13		
Stacey	30		70%	
Carly	36		75%	
Judy	26			50%
Fay	25			40%

18 Use squared paper. Draw an 8 × 5 grid of 40 boxes.
   a) Put ticks in 25% of the boxes.
   b) Put crosses in 40% of the boex.
   c) Put circles in 15% of the boxes.

On this page you will learn to find percentages of numbers.

Examples

$$75\% \text{ of } 60 = \tfrac{3}{4} \text{ of } 60 \qquad 30\% \text{ of } 40 = \tfrac{3}{10} \text{ of } 40$$
$$\tfrac{1}{4} \text{ of } 60 = 15 \qquad \tfrac{1}{10} \text{ of } 40 = 4$$
$$\tfrac{3}{4} \text{ or } 75\% \text{ of } 60 = 45 \qquad \tfrac{3}{10} \text{ or } 30\% \text{ of } 40 = 12$$

A

Work out

1. 10% of 70
2. 50% of 42
3. 25% of 24
4. 10% of 150

5. 20% of 35
6. 30% of 160
7. 75% of 60
8. 40% of 30

9. 10% of 130
10. 50% of 500
11. 20% of 250
12. 25% of 40

13. 20% of 15
14. 30% of 400
15. 40% of 50
16. 75% of 120

17. There were 130 apples in a barrel. 10% were rotten. How many apples were rotten?

18. 25% of the 240 passengers on a plane had not flown before. How many passengers had flown before?

B

Work out

1. 10% of 55
2. 20% of 180
3. 25% of 96
4. 40% of 22

5. 50% of 19
6. 30% of 140
7. 1% of 430
8. 70% of 60

9. 20% of 85
10. 75% of 320
11. 80% of 110
12. 1% of 37

13. 60% of 120
14. 90% of 150
15. 1% of 2000
16. 5% of 50

17. A baker made 64 cakes. 75% were sold. How many cakes were left?

18. There are 180 children in a school. 30% have milk every day. How many children do not have milk?

C

1. There were 240 children in a school. 60% were boys. How many girls were there?

2. 75% of the children in a class could swim. This was 21 children. How many children were there in the class?

3. 30% of the children in Year 6 belonged to the Guitar Club. This was 12 children. How many children were in Year 6?

4. Ian weighed 60 kg. His weight increased by 5%. What was his new weight?

5. A test had 80 questions. Amy correctly answered 85%. How many questions did she not answer correctly?

6. There were 300 children at a concert. 45% were girls. How many were boys?

On this page you will solve simple problems involving ratio and proportion.

A

A department store's loyalty card entitles the customer to a discount of one pound in every £50 spent. Copy and complete the table.

1

Amount spent (£s)	50	100	150							
Discount (£s)	1			4	5	6	7	8	9	10

2 Make a similar table for a discount of £1 in every £30 spent.

B

Copy and complete these sentences for each of the patterns below.
Write both sentences for each pattern.

1 **2** **3** **4** **5** **6**

a) The ratio of shaded squares to white squares is ☐ to every ☐.
b) The proportion of shaded squares in the pattern is ☐. (Write a fraction.)

C

1 There are nine girls to every four boys at a swimming pool.
There are 16 boys at the pool. How many girls are there?

2 For every five adults on a bus there are three children.
There are 21 children on the bus. How many adults are there?

3 400 people attend a concert. There are seven children to every three adults. How many children are at the concert?

4 One in every thirty raffle tickets won a prize.
There were 600 tickets sold. How many tickets won prizes?

5 In a test Rachel answered seven questions correctly to every five she answered wrongly.
There were 60 questions in the test. How many did she get right?

6 There are 36 chocolates in a box. Four in every nine have soft centres.
How many chocolates have hard centres?

7 In an orchard there are 5 times as many apple trees as there are pear trees.
There are 300 trees in the orchard altogether. How many pear trees are there?

8 A jeweller mends 7 watches for every 2 he sells.
In one month he mends 56 watches. How many does he sell?

On these pages you will learn:

- to find percentages of amounts of money.

Examples

$$90\% \text{ of } £6·00 = \frac{9}{10} \text{ of } £6·00$$

$$\frac{1}{10} \text{ of } £6·00 = 60p$$

$$\frac{9}{10} \text{ or } 90\% \text{ of } £6·00 = £5·40$$

- to find percentages by halving.

Example

Find 62·5% of £500

100% of £500 = £500

50% of £500 = £250

25% of £500 = £125

12·5% of £500 = £62·50

62·5% of £500 = £250 + £62·50

= £312·50

 A

For each of the following items in a sale, find:

a) the amount the price is reduced.

b) the new price.

1
SUITS
£100·00

10% OFF

5
TROUSERS
£15·00

20% OFF

9
COATS
£40·00

25% OFF

2
GLOVES
£5·00

50% OFF

6
TIES
£3·60

10% OFF

10
SHIRTS
£10·00

40% OFF

3
SOCKS
£2·40

25% OFF

7
TRAINERS
£20·00

30% OFF

11
SHOES
£25·00

20% OFF

4
BELTS
£8·50

10% OFF

8
HATS
£8

20% OFF

12
SCARVES
£6·00

25% OFF

Work out 75% of the following amounts of money by halving.

13 £1·20   **14** 40p   **15** £30·00   **16** 92p   **17** £2·20   **18** £68·00

B

Copy and complete the table.

1

Item	Price	Sale price 10% Discount	Sale price 5% Discount	Sale price 20% Discount	Sale price 30% Discount
Tennis racket	£30·00	£27·00			
Tennis balls	£3·60				
Football	£18·00				
Laces	£1·20				
Snooker table	£240·00				
Chalk	40p				
Cricket ball	£6·40				
Stumps		£8·10			

Work out 12·5% of the following amounts of money by halving.

2 72p   **3** £10·00   **4** £1·20   **5** £3·60   **6** £25·20   **7** £12·24

C

Find the odd one out in each set.

1 40% of 75p
10% of £30
3% of £10

2 5% of £8·40
6% of £7·00
25% of £1·60

3 20% of £3·20
1% of £32·00
32% of £2·00

4 5% of £3·80
2% of £9·50
20% of 90p

5 Copy and complete the table.

PRICE	SALE PRICE 15% DISCOUNT
£10·00	£8·50
£0·60	
£250·00	
£4·80	
£180·00	
£15·00	
£3·40	
£8·00	
£220·00	
£16·00	

6 Value Added Tax (VAT) is charged on many items at $17\frac{1}{2}$%. $17\frac{1}{2}$% can be calculated by halving.

Example

$17\frac{1}{2}$% of £500·00

10% of £500 = £50·00
5% of £500 = £25·00
$2\frac{1}{2}$% of £500 = £12·50
$17\frac{1}{2}$% of £500 = £87·50

Use this method to find $17\frac{1}{2}$% of:
a) £60·00   d) £76·00
b) £10·80   e) £124·00
c) £4·40   f) £15·20

PRICES SLASHED

On this page you will learn to understand the vocabulary and operation of addition.

2175 + 396 can be expressed in different ways.

the sum of 2175 and 396	2175 add 396
the total of 2175 and 396	2175 plus 396
2175 and 396 added together	396 greater than 2175
2175 increased by 396	396 more than 2175.

A

Work out

1 67 plus 67.

2 234 add 48.

3 The sum of 1·6 and 1·7.

4 148 increased by 71.

5 500 more than 837.

6 The total of 168 and 96.

7 629 and 240 added together.

8 170 greater than 180.

9 59 added to 256.

10 428 plus 350.

11 48 increased by 46.

12 400 greater than 713.

B

Copy and complete by writing the missing number in the box.

1 The total of 2·73 and ☐ is 3.

2 0·36 greater than ☐ is 0·96.

3 4600 add ☐ is 8200.

4 3700 plus ☐ is 5500.

5 ☐ more than 6·71 is 6·8.

6 ☐ and 2·4 added together is 5·69.

7 5·43 increased by ☐ is 5·5.

8 The sum of 3·48 and ☐ is 4.

9 3600 added to ☐ is 7100.

10 The total of 0·35 and ☐ is 0·65.

11 0·29 greater than ☐ is 0·79.

12 ☐ plus 3·1 is 9·5.

C

Copy and complete by writing the missing number in the box.

1 1·759 + ☐ = 2

2 6700 + ☐ = 12 300

3 ☐ + 0·043 = 1·2

4 7800 + ☐ = 15 200

5 2·183 + ☐ = 2·19

6 ☐ + 0·035 = 1

7 3·564 + ☐ = 3·6

8 6900 + ☐ = 11 400

9 ☐ + 0·382 = 4

10 0·683 + ☐ = 0·7

11 0·154 + ☐ = 0·16

12 ☐ + 5600 = 13 200

13 Find all the different totals you can make using three of these five numbers.

0·703   0·73   0·3   30·7   7·37

On this page you will learn to understand the vocabulary and operation of subtraction.

SUBTRACTION IS:

TAKING AWAY.	FINDING A DIFFERENCE.
7 take away 3.	The difference between 7 and 3.
7 subtract 3.	How many more is 7 than 3?
7 decreased by 3.	How many less is 3 than 7?

THE INVERSE OF ADDITION.

Find the missing number. $\Box - 0.39 = 0.4$

The answer is 0.79 because $0.4 + 0.39 = 0.79$.

A

Work out

1. Take 0·7 from 1.
2. 601 subtract 395.
3. 41 less than 896.
4. 5 decreased by 4·6.

5. 1438 take away 500.
6. Subtract 2·7 from 6·4.
7. 420 less than 756.
8. 6005 take 4997.

9. Decrease 540 by 280.
10. 10 subtract 4·8.
11. 0·35 less than 0·83.
12. 353 take away 29.

B

Copy and complete by writing the missing number in the box.

1. $\Box$ take 0·6 is 0·24.
2. 7000 take $\Box$ is 3146.
3. $\Box$ decreased by 0·4 is 0·06.
4. 0·8 decreased by $\Box$ is 0·46.
5. $\Box$ is 2600 less than 4200.
6. 2·3 is $\Box$ more than 1·4.

7. $\Box$ subtract 0·48 is 0·1.
8. 8200 subtract $\Box$ is 3700.
9. $\Box$ take away 0·23 is 0·7.
10. 6 take away $\Box$ is 0·63.
11. $\Box$ is 800 more than 3700.
12. 6·7 is $\Box$ more than 2·1.

C

Find the difference between these numbers and the target number.

$\boxed{10}$		$\boxed{1}$		$\boxed{0.49}$
1 5·8	5 0·28	9 1·65		
2 9·19	6 0·523	10 5·72		
3 4·76	7 0·918	11 3·8		
4 1·32	8 0·761	12 0·513		

Copy and complete.

13. $\Box - 2800 = 7600$
14. $0.118 - \Box = 0.098$
15. $\Box - 0.4 = 0.318$
16. $12\,300 - \Box = 5800$
17. $\Box - 0.36 = 0.029$

18. $0.621 - \Box = 0.321$
19. $\Box - 8700 = 3400$
20. $0.547 - \Box = 0.337$
21. $\Box - 0.417 = 0.583$
22. $14\,200 - \Box = 6600$

On this page you will learn to find a difference by counting up through the next multiple of 10, 100 or 1000.

Examples

$403 - 186 = 4 + 10 + 200 + 3 = 217$
$7003 - 3995 = 5 + 3000 + 3 = 3008$
$8000 - 2785 = 5 + 10 + 200 + 5000 = 5215$

A

Work out

1 $604 - 396$
2 $706 - 299$
3 $908 - 569$
4 $803 - 285$
5 $6000 - 2994$
6 $5000 - 1976$
7 $8000 - 5963$
8 $7000 - 2959$
9 $6007 - 3995$
10 $9003 - 4998$

B

Work out

1 $801 - 587$
2 $726 - 169$
3 $635 - 272$
4 $542 - 184$
5 $8000 - 3887$
6 $6000 - 3655$
7 $6007 - 2984$
8 $9008 - 4963$
9 $7014 - 4995$
10 $8016 - 2979$

C

Copy and complete.

1 $8100 - \square = 2776$
2 $7200 - \square = 3892$
3 $6300 - \square = 3765$
4 $9100 - \square = 4688$
5 $9300 - \square = 4855$
6 $7400 - \square = 3764$
7 $8200 - \square = 2687$
8 $6200 - \square = 2768$
9 $7050 - \square = 1940$
10 $6040 - \square = 2960$

Now you will learn to identify near doubles.

Examples

$317 + 284 = (300 \times 2) + 17 - 16 = 600 + 1 = 601$
$20 \cdot 4 + 19 \cdot 7 = (20 \times 2) + 0 \cdot 4 - 0 \cdot 3 = 40 + 0 \cdot 1 = 40 \cdot 1$

A

Work out

1 $46 + 53$
2 $57 + 61$
3 $79 + 84$
4 $68 + 72$
5 $29 + 32$
6 $65 + 73$
7 $3 \cdot 5 + 3 \cdot 7$
8 $2 \cdot 2 + 2 \cdot 4$
9 $4 \cdot 5 + 4 \cdot 4$
10 $4 \cdot 1 + 3 \cdot 8$

B

Work out

1 $302 + 294$
2 $413 + 391$
3 $387 + 415$
4 $484 + 522$
5 $197 + 206$
6 $492 + 516$
7 $2 \cdot 7 + 2 \cdot 8$
8 $4 \cdot 9 + 4 \cdot 8$
9 $5 \cdot 4 + 4 \cdot 7$
10 $6 \cdot 2 + 5 \cdot 9$

C

Copy and complete.

1 $\square - 19 \cdot 6 = 20 \cdot 7$
2 $\square - 50 \cdot 8 = 49 \cdot 5$
3 $\square - 25 \cdot 6 = 24 \cdot 8$
4 $\square - 31 \cdot 4 = 29 \cdot 3$
5 $\square - 18 \cdot 7 = 21 \cdot 6$
6 $\square - 41 \cdot 2 = 39 \cdot 9$
7 $\square - 38 \cdot 5 = 42 \cdot 9$
8 $\square - 38 \cdot 3 = 42 \cdot 5$
9 $\square - 34 \cdot 7 = 35 \cdot 6$
10 $\square - 57 \cdot 8 = 61 \cdot 3$

On this page you will learn to add or subtract to the nearest whole number and adjust.

Examples

$4.5 + 3.9 = 4.5 + 4.0 - 0.1 = 8.5 - 0.1 = 8.4$

$7.8 - 2.9 = 7.8 - 3.0 + 0.1 = 4.8 + 0.1 = 4.9$

$4.3 - 2.1 = 4.3 - 2.0 - 0.1 = 2.3 - 0.1 = 2.2$

A

Work out

1 $1.5 + 0.9$
2 $6.2 - 0.9$
3 $7.1 + 1.1$
4 $3.9 - 1.1$
5 $2.3 + 0.9$
6 $4.5 - 0.9$
7 $3.5 + 1.1$
8 $2.6 - 1.1$
9 $4.8 + 0.9$
10 $5.4 - 0.9$

B

Work out

1 $1.6 + 0.9$
2 $7.3 - 1.9$
3 $6.8 + 2.1$
4 $7.6 - 1.1$
5 $3.7 + 2.9$
6 $6.4 - 0.9$
7 $3.7 + 4.1$
8 $3.3 - 3.1$
9 $4.8 + 3.9$
10 $5.5 - 2.9$

C

Copy and complete.

1 $\square - 19.6 = 20.7$
2 $\square - 50.8 = 49.6$
3 $\square - 40.4 = 39.2$
4 $\square - 29.3 = 31.4$
5 $\square - 21.6 = 18.7$
6 $\square - 48.3 = 52.1$
7 $\square - 38.5 = 42.9$
8 $\square - 42.5 = 38.3$
9 $\square - 71.2 = 68.7$
10 $\square - 57.8 = 61.3$

Now you will learn to use the relationship between addition and subtraction.

If you know one addition or subtraction fact you can state three other related facts.

Example

$3.32 - 2.53 = 0.79 \quad 3.32 - 0.79 = 2.53$

$2.53 + 0.79 = 3.32 \quad 0.79 + 2.53 = 3.32$

A

Copy and complete. Use the 3 given numbers only.

1 $67 + 74 = 141$
   $74 + \square = \square$
   $141 - \square = \square$
   $\square - \square = \square$

2 $4.7 + 1.1 = \square$
   $\square + \square = \square$
   $\square - \square = 1.1$
   $5.8 - \square = \square$

3 $153 + 27 = \square$
   $\square + \square = 180$
   $\square - 27 = \square$
   $\square - \square = \square$

B

Work out and write three other related facts.

1 $1.64 + 3.9$
2 $5.7 - 3.1$
3 $3.7 + 5.9$
4 $6.8 - 2.4$
5 $0.07 + 0.3$
6 $2001 - 240$
7 $3016 + 1994$
8 $4007 - 1983$
9 $6004 + 2997$
10 $9200 - 5800$

C

For each set of numbers write four related + or − facts.

1 $3.6, 5.47, 9.07$
2 $3.4, 1.7, 5.1$
3 $4003, 1022, 2981$
4 $2986, 6021, 3007$
5 $3.8, 6.51, 2.71$
6 $6.4, 3.8, 2.6$
7 $2965, 4049, 7014$
8 $9048, 3975, 5023$
9 $2.83, 6.6, 3.77$
10 $4.54, 0.56, 5.1$

On this page you will learn to use a variety of strategies to add several numbers.

Examples

Look for pairs that make multiples of 10 or 100.

$$20 + 70 + 80 = 80 + 20 + 70$$
$$= 100 + 70$$
$$= 170$$

Start with the largest number.

$$6 + 13 + 28 + 5 = 28 + 13 + 6 + 5$$
$$= 41 + 6 + 5$$
$$= 47 + 5$$
$$= 52$$

Recognise an equivalent multiplication.

$$14 + 15 + 16 + 15 = 4 \times 15$$
$$= 60$$

There are ten ways of going from the Start to the Finish.

Find the total for each of the ten routes.

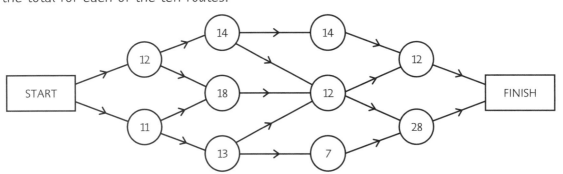

B

Work out

1. $26 + 18 + 14 + 7$
2. $21 + 23 + 24 + 22$
3. $30 + 50 + 60 + 50$
4. $52 + 50 + 53 + 57$
5. $90 + 70 + 20 + 40$

6. $28 + 27 + 16 + 22$
7. $15 + 19 + 25 + 17$
8. $7 + 6 + 18 + 5 + 9$
9. $5 + 14 + 9 + 6 + 3$
10. $38 + 24 + 32 + 13$

11. $15 + 9 + 24 + 7$
12. $9 + 5 + 13 + 7 + 8$
13. $39 + 38 + 39 + 40$
14. $40 + 30 + 50 + 70$
15. $50 + 190 + 30 + 80$

C

Copy and complete by writing the missing number in the box.

1. $76 + 18 + \square + 34 = 144$
2. $50 + 40 + \square + 60 + 20 = 260$
3. $40 + 39 + \square + 42 + 41 = 205$
4. $72 + \square + 39 + 48 = 187$
5. $140 + 270 + \square + 160 = 720$

6. $59 + \square + 43 + 61 = 199$
7. $6 + 18 + \square + 27 + 62 = 130$
8. $30 + 240 + 170 + \square = 510$
9. $24 + 25 + 28 + \square + 27 = 130$
10. $90 + 70 + 480 + \square + 40 = 740$

On this page you will use and explain a variety of strategies to add or subtract pairs of numbers mentally.

A

Copy and complete the squares.

1

+	260	380	450
390	650		
540			
460			

2

−	320	250	510
873	553		
685			
968			

3

+	2·6	1·9	5·7
2·5			
3·7			
5·8			

4

−	360	290	470
540			
820			
650			

5

+	700	500	800
693			
879			
521			

6

−	2·6	5·9	4·8
8·2	5·6		
7·5			
9·3			

B

Write the answers only.

1 $6800 + 2500$

2 $5300 - 2700$

3 $0·5 + 0·28$

4 $0·72 - 0·4$

5 $0·65 + 0·3$

6 $0·9 - 0·32$

7 $3600 + 3500$

8 $3·2 - 0·05$

9 $0·04 + 0·2$

10 $0·6 - 0·17$

11 $3700 + 4800$

12 $9300 - 4700$

13 $0·4 + 0·31$

14 $0·84 - 0·6$

15 $0·53 + 0·4$

16 $8100 - 2900$

Add 5·9 to:

17 3·7

18 5·4

19 8·9

Add 3600 to:

20 2600

21 5900

22 4700

Take 3·1 from:

23 6·5

24 9·2

25 4·8

Take 2700 from:

26 7400

27 3600

28 9100

Make 1.

29 0·54

30 0·37

31 0·61

Make 10 000.

32 7300

33 5800

34 1400

C

Copy and complete.

1 $\square + 4700 = 11\,500$

2 $\square - 6900 = 5400$

3 $0·524 - \square = 0·124$

4 $\square - 0·006 = 0·065$

5 $\square + 0·3 = 0·796$

6 $0·951 - \square = 0·948$

7 $2·681 + \square = 3$

8 $2·681 + \square = 2·7$

9 $2·681 + \square = 2·69$

10 $0·892 - \square = 0·592$

11 $\square - 0·877 = 1$

12 $\square - 0·344 = 0·4$

13 $\square - 0·253 = 0·26$

14 $0·68 - \square = 0·674$

15 $0·8 - \square = 0·725$

16 $\square + 3400 = 11\,100$

17 $\square - 4300 = 8800$

18 $7500 + \square = 13\,300$

Copy and complete the squares.

19

+	0·38	0·9	1·06
0·67			
1·5			
2·4			

20

−	0·5	0·38	0·76
1·0	0·5		
2·6			
0·82			

On this page you will learn two informal methods for addition.

ADD LARGEST VALUE DIGITS FIRST

Examples	5384	2673
	+2729	+1592
	7000	3000
	1000	1100
	100	160
	13	5
	8113	4265

COMPENSATION

Example	4865	
	+2678	
	7865	(4865 + 3000)
	− 322	(2678 − 3000)
	7543	

A

Use both methods for each sum.

1. 583 + 249
6. 364 + 186

2. 659 + 278
7. 786 + 275

3. 871 + 685
8. 947 + 593

4. 1654 + 927
9. 1368 + 467

5. 2087 + 359
10. 4923 + 958

11. 267 women and 395 men belong to a Health Club. How many members are there altogether?

B

Use both methods for each sum.

1. 4287 + 1946
6. 4392 + 4678

2. 3649 + 1578
7. 2685 + 1594

3. 4564 + 2788
8. 5417 + 2863

4. 6478 + 1957
9. 7254 + 4135

5. 5895 + 2578
10. 8769 + 3946

11. In December a factory made 5962 cars. In January production increased by 1378. How many cars were made in January?

12. Aeysha's annual salary was £17 348. She also earned a bonus of £1365. How much was she paid altogether?

C

Add largest value digits first. Set out as in the examples.

1. 3486 + 1957
2. 12 385 + 7850
3. 23 408 + 15 473
4. 9748 + 2976
5. 5839 + 7794
6. 38 674 + 9369

Use compensation. Set out as in the example.

7. 6907 + 5798
8. 7564 + 3988
9. 47 561 + 24 938
10. 8675 + 4976
11. 17 923 + 5786
12. 56 790 + 7692
13. A car had a mileage of 32 517. In the next year it was driven a further 9864 miles. What was the new mileage?

On this page you will learn to use a standard method for addition.

Examples

```
   643          3248          7486
 + 428        +1572        + 3927
 ─────        ─────        ──────
  1071         4820         11413
    1            11          1 11
```

A

Copy and complete.

1. 485
   +348

7. 3682
   + 469

2. 379
   +184

8. 1568
   + 785

3. 696
   +275

9. 4574
   + 972

4. 1257
   + 596

10. 2871
    + 854

5. 2808
   + 639

11. 3695
    + 637

6. 2937
   + 448

12. 5284
    + 919

13. 2758 cars used a car park on Sunday. This was 697 fewer cars than on the previous day. How many cars had used the car park on Saturday?

B

Copy and complete.

1. 4835
   +2689

7. 9837
   +1695

2. 5786
   +3698

8. 6794
   +5987

3. 7968
   +4287

9. 7985
   +4653

4. 6957
   +5728

10. 9469
    +5165

5. 3579
   +1859

11. 8736
    +3295

6. 8658
   +1879

12. 7689
    +5726

13. Winston has £6584 in his bank account. A cheque for his monthly salary of £1947 is paid in. How much is there now in the account?

14. New York is 3473 miles from London. San Francisco is a further 1896 miles away. How far is it from London to San Francisco?

C

Set out as in the example.

1. 13 756 + 8475
2. 24 673 + 6959
3. 51 968 + 8274
4. 84 789 + 7689
5. 60 597 + 5768
6. 29 627 + 4896
7. 58 384 + 3876
8. 47 493 + 5876
9. 36 569 + 9653
10. 43 758 + 8974

11. The population of a town is 69 776. A further 6478 people live in a nearby village. What is their combined population?

12. 35 827 watched City's home game. The attendance at their next match was 9 195 more. How many people watched the second game?

On this page you will learn:

- **to add several numbers.**

Example

Add 7, 638, 2614, 92, 3526

```
      7
    638    Line-up
   2614    the units.
     92
  +3526
  ─────
   6877
   1 1 2
```

- **to add decimals.**

Example

320 m + 5·7 km + 83 m

```
      km
   0·320    Line up the
   5·700    decimal points.
  +0·083    Put in missing zeros.
  ──────
   6·103
    1 1
```

A

Copy and complete.

1
```
    26
   488
     3
  1265
  +  97
```

2
```
   329
    59
  3642
    47
  +   8
```

3
```
  2406
    75
   186
     4
  +  83
```

4
```
     £
  1·63
  0·28
  0·07
  +1·15
```

5
```
     £
  4·38
  1·92
  0·06
  +2·54
```

6
```
     £
  0·32
  3·46
  2·59
  +1·01
```

B

Set out as sums and find the totals.

1 324 + 4452 + 56 + 8 + 1705

2 3663 + 3 + 971 + 2537 + 79

3 2192 + 586 + 3675 + 98 + 2

4 5 + 1738 + 27 + 243 + 2584

5 23·29 + 6·8

6 145·7 + 2·38

7 18·2 + 1·03 + 0·25

8 217·16 + 0·05 + 3·7

9 1·3 km + 270 m

10 4·86 km + 1300 m

11 400 m + 60 m + 2·7 km

12 0·8 km + 4·365 km + 20 m

C

Set out as sums and find the totals.

1 182 + 3254 + 736 + 3 + 12 387

2 6 + 30 653 + 541 + 3475 + 928

3 2963 + 345 + 25712 + 294 + 7

4 57 919 + 683 + 8 + 2537 + 651

5 6·1 + 0·087

6 13·04 + 7·603

7 1·92 + 148·3 + 0·165

8 17·36 + 1·128 + 0·9

9 12·1 km + 263 m

10 0·07 km + 1832 m

11 1·3 km + 0·97 km + 156 m

12 0·006 km + 19 m + 7 m

On this page you will learn two informal written methods for subtraction.

COUNTING UP

```
  5435
− 1767
─────
    33   (1800)
   200   (2000)
  3435   (5435)
─────
  3668
```

COMPENSATION

```
  5345
− 1767
─────
  3345   (5345 − 2000)
+  233   (2000 − 1767)
─────
  3578
```

A

Use both methods for each sum.

1   437   **7**   361
       − 186   − 289

2   293   **8**   953
       − 175   − 564

3   359   **9**   237
       − 268   − 178

4   565   **10**   872
       − 437   − 317

5   681   **11**   540
       − 394   − 181

6   724   **12**   913
       − 255   − 625

13 Glen spent £625 on hats on Friday and £382 on Saturday. How much less did he spend on Saturday?

B

Use both methods for each sum.

1   2961   **7**   6315
       − 1397   − 3678

2   5146   **8**   5873
       − 3972   − 4132

3   8362   **9**   3140
       − 2784   − 2753

4   6314   **10**   7522
       − 2586   − 3947

5   9083   **11**   8305
       − 4430   − 5863

6   4160   **12**   9141
       − 2381   − 2703

13 There are 1267 children in Southan. The population of the town is 8254. How many adults live in the town?

14 8651 people saw a film in June. 2174 less people saw the film in July. What was the total audience for July?

C

Set out correctly. Use both methods for each sum.

1 16 512 − 14 675

2 13 747 − 12 968

3 27 934 − 18 157

4 32 158 − 25 389

5 50 361 − 33 596

6 24 061 − 17 596

7 37 517 − 29 831

8 46 234 − 18 359

9 48 902 − 23 145

10 31 185 − 24 637

11 42 350 − 22 576

12 60 713 − 39 816

13 In her old job Amelia was paid £17 956 each year. Her new annual salary is £24 172. By how much has her salary increased?

14 52 750 copies of a magazine were printed but only 38 519 were sold. How many copies were not sold?

On this page you will learn to use decomposition.

METHOD 1

$$5428 = 53^12 8 = 4^13^12 8$$
$$-2794 \qquad -2794 \qquad -2794$$
$$\qquad\qquad\qquad\qquad\qquad\qquad 2 6 3 4$$

METHOD 2

$$\overset{4\ \ 13\ 12}{\cancel{5}\cancel{4}\cancel{2}8}$$
$$-2794$$
$$\overline{2634}$$

A

Use Method 1.

1 374   **4** 737
     −168   −293

2 485   **5** 529
     −237   −438

3 609   **6** 850
     −345   −471

Use Method 2.

7 638   **10** 426
     −276   −218

8 394   **11** 923
     −167   −456

9 251   **12** 841
     −139   −537

13 Arthur worked for 325 minutes on Monday and only 183 minutes on Tuesday. How many more minutes did he work on Monday?

B

Use Method 2.

1 4080   **7** 5832
     −2163   −2563

2 2737   **8** 3690
     −1943   −2318

3 5326   **9** 9416
     −2851   −5738

4 7143   **10** 8025
     −3456   −3279

5 3501   **11** 6174
     −2937   −4586

6 8264   **12** 7350
     −3895   −6974

13 Mustapha has £2640 in his bank account. He withdraws £1825. How much is left in the account?

14 In one week 1827 children used a swimming pool. The total number of tickets sold was 3163. How many adults used the pool?

C

Set out correctly and use Method 2.

1 43 464 − 13 709

2 32 032 − 16 158

3 20 783 − 10 795

4 45 327 − 26 587

5 51 501 − 24 653

6 74 260 − 47 898

7 34 715 − 16 379

8 53 263 − 24 685

9 71 521 − 42 763

10 42 170 − 39 186

11 25 312 − 17 615

12 80 637 − 53 789

13 In December a shop had takings of £51 309. In January takings fell by £23 687. How much was taken in January?

14 At the beginning of the year the milometer on a car read 27 495. At the end of the year it read 42 360. How many miles had the car travelled during the year?

On this page you will learn:

● to find the difference between numbers with different numbers of digits.

Example

Find the difference
between 3268 and 29 475.

```
  29475    Larger number on top
−  3268    Line up the units.
```

● to find the difference between decimals.

Example

Find the difference
between 2·47 and 0·6.

```
  2·47    Line up the decimal points.
− 0·60    Put in missing zeros.
```

A

Copy and complete.

1
```
  5136
−   93
```

2
```
  3462
−  247
```

3
```
  1271
−  368
```

4
```
  4053
−  527
```

5
```
  6514
−   47
```

6
```
  7320
−  264
```

7
```
  7·35
− 5·69
```

8
```
  4·20
− 1·37
```

9
```
  8·41
− 4·38
```

10
```
  43·1
− 16·5
```

11 A shop has 1352 pairs of shoes in stock.
639 pairs are sold.
How many are left?

12 A plank is 3·25 metres long. 1·38 metres is sawn off. How long is the plank now?

B

Set out correctly and find the differences.

1 12 632 and 1374

2 687 and 35 410

3 20 371 and 2193

4 1761 and 57 143

5 41 528 and 571

6 698 and 63 250

7 26·1 − 1·8

8 80·2 − 13·75

9 45·3 − 9·7

10 4·22 − 2·5

11 3·5 − 0·61

12 2·4 − 1·55

13 The 100 metres was won in 10·83 seconds. Justin's time was 11·4 seconds. What was the difference between Justin's time and the winner's time?

C

Set out correctly and find the differences.

1 135 703 and 981

2 687 and 35 410

3 20 371 and 2193

4 1761 and 57 143

5 41 528 and 571

6 698 and 63 250

7 14·32 − 1·5

8 3·21 − 0·526

9 4·391 − 2·7

10 8·13 − 1·64

11 27·4 − 4·965

12 3·625 − 0·79

13 Iqbal has £17 243 in his bank account. He withdraws £1864. How much is left in the account?

14 A lorry is carrying 2·3 tonnes of goods. 0·56 tonnes is unloaded. How much weight is the lorry carrying?

On this page you will learn to use the inverse relationship of multiplication and division.

Example

Knowing one × or ÷ fact means that you know 3 related facts.

$0.4 \times 6 = 2.4$ $6 \times 0.4 = 2.4$
$2.4 \div 6 = 0.4$ $2.4 \div 0.4 = 6$

A

Copy and complete each table.

1

×6	
9	→ 54
0·1	→
	→ 2·4
	→ 3·6
8	→

2

×7	
8	→ 56
	→ 42
0·5	→
	→ 6·3
0·3	→

3

×8	
5	→ 40
0·6	→
	→ 7·2
	→ 56
	→ 3·2

4

×9	
0·2	→ 1·8
	→ 81
	→ 4·5
	→ 63
0·6	→

B

Copy and complete.

1 ☐ × 0·25 = 4

2 4 × ☐ = 2·8

3 ☐ × 2·3 = 23

4 7 × ☐ = 0·07

5 ☐ × 0·5 = 10

6 ☐ × 1 = 3

7 6 × ☐ = 0

8 ☐ × 8 = 6·4

9 4 × ☐ = 0·36

10 ☐ × 0·3 = 2·1

11 ☐ × 100 = 90

12 3 × ☐ = 0·15

13 ☐ × 5 = 2·0

14 0·9 × ☐ = 0·9

15 ☐ × 6 = 0·48

Write four different × or ÷ statements for each set of numbers.

16 1·2, 0·4, 3

17 0·2, 7, 1·4

18 6·5, 5, 1·3

19 2, 1·6, 3·2

20 6, 4, 1·5

21 0·7, 2·5, 1·75

22 1·9, 3, 5·7

23 0·6, 8·4, 14

24 80, 400, 5

C

Copy and complete these multiplication squares.

1
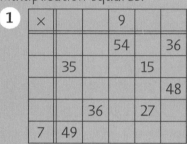

×			9	
			54	36
	35		15	
				48
		36	27	
7	49			

2
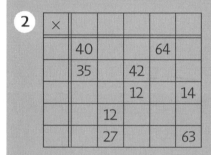

×				
	40		64	
	35	42		
			12	14
		12		
		27		63

3
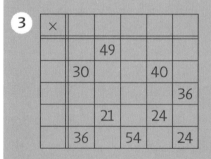

×				
		49		
	30		40	
				36
	21		24	
	36		54	24

4
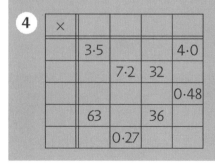

×				
	3·5			4·0
		7·2	32	
				0·48
	63		36	
		0·27		

MULTIPLICATION PROBLEMS

On this page you will learn to use the vocabulary of multiplication.

A

Write a number sentence for each problem and then work out the answer.

1. Find 7 groups of 6.
2. What is 20 times greater than 9?
3. What is 9 multiplied by 7?
4. Find the product of 31 and 8.
5. Multiply 0·4 by 10.
6. What is 3 times 1·5?
7. There are 16 biscuits in a packet. There are 5 packets. How many biscuits are there?
8. A small box holds 80 tea bags. A larger box holds three times as many. How many tea bags are in the larger box?
9. A shelf holds 15 videos. How many videos can 15 shelves hold?
10. It takes Navid 7·4 seconds to walk 10 metres. How long will it take him to walk 100 metres?

B

Write a number sentence for each problem and work out the answer.

1. Find the product of 5 and 19.
2. What is 0·08 times 10?
3. Multiply 75 by 8.
4. What is 5 groups of 0·6?
5. An ant takes 1·23 seconds to walk 1 cm. How long will it take the ant to walk 2 metres?
6. How many hours are there in a week?
7. There are 17 oak trees in a wood. There are eight times as many beech trees. How many beech trees are there in the wood?
8. 300 people watch a film on Thursday. The audience on Friday is 1·6 times larger. How many people watch the film on Friday?

THE END

C

1. Look at the numbers in the box.

0·2	2·5	0·8	0·25	1·4

   a) What is the largest number multiplied by the smallest number?
   b) What number is 1000 times greater than the second largest number?
   c) What is 13 lots of the middle number?
   d) Multiply the total of the three smallest numbers by 8.
   e) What is the square of the sum of the two largest numbers?
   f) Ten different products can be made using pairs of the five numbers. Can you find them all?

2. A play was performed 16 times. The average audience was 275. How many people saw the play?

3. Each stride Jessica takes is 0·8 metres long. She paces out 260 strides. How far has she walked?

On this page you will learn to use the inverse relationship of division to multiplication.

Example

Knowing one × or ÷ fact means that you know 3 related facts.

$8 \div 5 = 1.6$ $8 \div 1.6 = 5$

$5 \times 1.6 = 8$ $1.6 \times 5 = 8$

A

Copy and complete the tables.

1

÷6
24 → 4
48 →
→ 10
42 →
→ 3
54 →

2

÷25
50 → 2
100 →
→ 10
→ 7
200 →
125 →

3

÷9
54 → 6
27 →
→ 8
36 →
→ 7
→ 9

4

÷10
270 → 27
35 →
→ 2·4
→ 8
630 →
→ 11·7

B

Copy and complete.

1 $72 \div \square = 8$

2 $\square \div 10 = 0.47$

3 $6.3 \div \square = 0.7$

4 $\square \div 100 = 2.3$

5 $54 \div \square = 9$

6 $0.9 \div \square = 0.9$

7 $\square \div 1 = 100$

8 $15 \div \square = 2.5$

9 $\square \div 12 = 12$

10 $240 \div \square = 40$

11 $28 \div \square = 0.28$

12 $\square \div 4 = 0.6$

13 $19 \div \square = 1.9$

14 $\square \div 6 = 0.8$

15 $11 \div \square = 0.11$

16 $240 \div \square = 12$

17 $\square \div 2 = 0.75$

18 $1 \div \square = 0.01$

19 $\square \div 7 = 1.3$

20 $400 \div \square = 50$

Write three related × or ÷ statements.

21 $4 \times 0.2 = 0.8$

22 $3.9 \div 3 = 1.3$

23 $800 \div 25 = 32$

24 $16 \times 24 = 384$

C

Copy and complete the tables.

1

INPUT		OUTPUT
6·25	÷5	
0·04	÷10	
0·56	÷8	
	÷1	39
	÷100	0·2
4·2		0·7
5		0·005
0·8		0·2

2

INPUT		OUTPUT
420	÷1000	
6·5	÷5	
	÷10	0·86
	÷9	0·04
	÷15	4·0
0·8		0·008
7·1		7·1
0·54		0·09

3

INPUT		OUTPUT
58	÷1	
2·7	÷100	
	÷8	0·08
	÷1000	0·01
	÷15	0·04
0·6		0·06
3		1·5
39		0·039

On this page you will learn to use the vocabulary of division.

A

Write a number sentence for each problem and work out the answer.

1. Share 600 by 20.
2. What is one fifth of 90?
3. How many 8s are there in 72?
4. Divide 72 by 6.
5. What is 2100 divided by 7?
6. How many 15s go into 120?
7. Each box holds 6 cakes. How many boxes can be filled from 240 cakes?
8. £5·00 is shared between 4 friends. How much does each friend receive?
9. Luke's grandmother is 91. She is seven times as old as Luke. How old is Luke?
10. How many years are there in 84 months?
11. A council worker cut 90 cm of tape into 6 equal lengths. How long is each piece of tape?

B

Write a number sentence for each problem and work out the answer.

1. A party of 22 people paid £396 for theatre tickets. How much did each ticket cost?

2. 300 children are divided equally into 12 classes. How many children are there in each class?
3. Each glass has a capacity of 220 ml. How many glasses can be filled from 3 litres of fruit juice? How much fruit juice is left over?
4. 7 metres of ribbon is cut into 25 equal lengths. How long is each length?
5. 120 children were asked to choose their favourite day of the week. One third chose Saturday, one quarter chose Sunday and one eighth chose Friday. How many children chose a different day?

C

Write a number sentence for each problem and work out the answer.

1. A lottery prize of £2100 is shared between 15 people. How much does each person win?
2. The 48 tins of sardines in a box weigh 16·8 kg. How much does each tin weigh?
3. Each bag holds 16 satsumas. How many bags can be filled from 592 satsumas?
4. In a random check, police found that 1 car in every 18 had dangerously worn tyres. 432 cars were inspected. How many cars had worn tyres?
5. In a game of Fantasy Cricket, England scored 252 runs. Openers Gooch and Compton scored one third and one quarter of the runs, while Botham smashed one seventh of the total. How many runs were scored by the rest of the side?

MULTIPLICATION FACTS

On this page you will practise the multiplication and division facts.

A
Write the answers only.

1. 6×2
2. 10×2
3. 9×2
4. 7×2
5. 1×2
6. 8×2
7. 5×3
8. 6×3
9. 0×3
10. 8×3
11. 7×3
12. 9×3
13. 8×4
14. 1×4
15. 7×4
16. 9×4
17. 6×4
18. 10×4
19. 4×5
20. 8×5
21. 6×5
22. 0×5
23. 9×5
24. 7×5
25. 6×6
26. 10×6
27. 8×6
28. 4×6
29. 9×6
30. 7×6
31. 9×7
32. 6×7
33. 1×7
34. 8×7
35. 7×7
36. 5×7
37. 0×8
38. 7×8
39. 9×8
40. 3×8
41. 6×8
42. 8×8
43. 8×9
44. 5×9
45. 7×9
46. 9×9
47. 4×9
48. 6×9

49. Copy and complete the multiplication square.

×				
6		24		
	63		72	
	21	12		

B
Copy and complete each of the tables.

1. ×6
0.8 →
0.4 →
0.5 →
0.7 →
→ 0
→ 0.6
→ 5.4
→ 3.6

2. ×7
0.3 →
8 →
5 →
0.7 →
→ 7
→ 4.2
→ 6.3
→ 2.8

3. ×8
5 →
0.9 →
0.2 →
8 →
→ 4.8
→ 8
→ 3.2
→ 56

4. ×9
4 →
1 →
0.6 →
0.3 →
→ 81
→ 6.3
→ 0
→ 7.2

C
Write the answers only.

1. 0.8×4
2. 7×0.6
3. 0.5×0.9
4. 0.6×0.8
5. 0.06×6
6. 0.6×9
7. 3×0.8
8. 8×0.6
9. 0.7×0.7
10. 8×0.05
11. 0.6×0.9
12. 0.9×0.8
13. 7×0.03
14. 0.04×8
15. 0.8×7
16. 0.8×0.8
17. 9×0.4
18. 0.9×7
19. 0.07×6
20. 0.9×0.9

Copy and complete.

21. $\square \times 7 = 0.63$
22. $0.6 \times \square = 0.18$
23. $\square \div 9 = 0.8$
24. $0.18 \div \square = 0.06$
25. $\square \times 8 = 4.8$
26. $0.08 \times \square = 0.56$
27. $\square \div 5 = 9$
28. $6.3 \div \square = 0.7$
29. $\square \times 4 = 28$
30. $6 \times \square = 3.6$
31. $\square \div 8 = 0.08$
32. $2.8 \div \square = 0.4$
33. $\square \times 9 = 0.81$
34. $0.6 \times \square = 0.42$
35. $\square \div 6 = 0.9$
36. $0.56 \div \square = 0.08$

On this page you will learn to give a remainder as a fraction or as a decimal fraction.

Examples

$$94 \div 4 = 23\frac{2}{4} = 23 \cdot 5$$

$$\begin{array}{r} 23 \cdot 5 \\ 4)\overline{94 \cdot 0} \\ \underline{8} \qquad (2 \times 4) \\ 14 \\ \underline{12} \qquad (3 \times 4) \\ 2 \cdot 0 \\ \underline{2 \cdot 0} \qquad (0 \cdot 5 \times 4) \end{array}$$

$$18 \div 7 = 2\frac{4}{7} = 2 \cdot 6 \text{ (to 1 decimal place)}$$

$$\begin{array}{r} 2 \cdot 57 \text{ etc.} \\ 7)\overline{18 \cdot 00} \\ \underline{14} \qquad (2 \times 7) \\ 4 \cdot 0 \\ \underline{3 \cdot 5} \qquad (0 \cdot 5 \times 7) \\ 0 \cdot 50 \\ \underline{0 \cdot 49} \qquad (0 \cdot 7 \times 7) \\ \text{etc.} \end{array}$$

A

Give the answer as a fraction.

1. $91 \div 4$
2. $169 \div 10$
3. $35 \div 8$
4. $307 \div 25$
5. $56 \div 9$
6. $68 \div 5$
7. $35 \div 6$
8. $579 \div 100$
9. $60 \div 7$
10. $23 \div 8$

Give the answer as a decimal.

11. $147 \div 2$
12. $61 \div 4$
13. $83 \div 5$
14. $497 \div 10$
15. $71 \div 4$
16. $£5 \cdot 70 \div 2$
17. $£13 \cdot 20 \div 4$
18. $£43 \cdot 20 \div 5$
19. $£29 \cdot 00 \div 10$
20. $£11 \cdot 40 \div 4$

21. Five friends travel by coach. Their tickets cost £78 altogether. How much does one ticket cost?

22. A car holds 50 litres of petrol. How many litres are left when the petrol tank is one quarter full?

B

Give the answer as a fraction.

1. $107 \div 7$
2. $103 \div 8$
3. $131 \div 9$
4. $183 \div 11$
5. $73 \div 6$
6. $173 \div 8$
7. $2617 \div 100$
8. $131 \div 6$
9. $238 \div 9$
10. $180 \div 7$

Give the answer as a decimal. Round to one decimal place where appropriate.

11. $177 \div 10$
12. $72 \div 5$
13. $58 \div 4$
14. $122 \div 9$
15. $80 \div 3$
16. $132 \div 8$
17. $93 \div 7$
18. $107 \div 6$
19. $181 \div 8$
20. $238 \div 9$

21. 8 loads weigh 1730 kg. What does one load weigh in kilograms?

C

Copy and complete.

1. $\square \div 6 = 18\frac{5}{6}$
2. $\square \div 9 = 26\frac{4}{9}$
3. $\square \div 15 = 12\frac{7}{15}$
4. $\square \div 8 = 21\frac{7}{8}$
5. $\square \div 13 = 13\frac{5}{13}$
6. $\square \div 7 = 33\frac{5}{7}$
7. $\square \div 8 = 27\frac{5}{8}$
8. $\square \div 7 = 48\frac{3}{7}$
9. $\square \div 12 = 16\frac{7}{12}$
10. $\square \div 9 = 43\frac{2}{9}$

Give the answer as a decimal fraction. Where appropriate, round to one decimal place.

11. $73 \div 20$
12. $2432 \div 1000$
13. $11 \div 8$
14. $173 \div 7$
15. $150 \div 9$
16. $92 \div 25$
17. $386 \div 8$
18. $294 \div 12$

On this page you will learn to make sensible decisions about rounding up or down after division.

Examples

- How many £12 tickets
  can I buy with £187?

  $187 \div 12 = 15$ remainder 7

  Answer: 15 tickets can be bought.

- An egg box holds 12 eggs.
  How many boxes are needed for 187 eggs?

  $187 \div 12 = 15$ remainder 7

  Answer: 16 boxes are needed.

- Each jar holds 400 g of jam.
  How many jars can be filled from 5
  kilograms of jam?

  $5000 \div 400 = 12$ remainder 200

  Answer: 12 jars can be filled.

- Maurice earns £400 each week.
  How many weeks will it take him to earn
  £5000?

  $5000 \div 400 = 12$ remainder 200

  Answer: It takes 13 weeks.

A

1. How many 7-a-side rugby teams can be formed from 95 players?

2. A shop can display 12 dresses on a rail. How many rails are needed to display 80 dresses?

3. 8 shuttlecocks are packed in a tube. How many tubes can be filled from 125 shuttlecocks?

4. 6 people can sit at each table in a factory canteen. How many tables are needed to seat the 200 workers at the factory?

5. A cup of coffee costs 90p. How many can be bought with £14?

6. Tom wants to buy a Hi Fi costing £150. He saves £9 each week. How many weeks will it take him to save the money he needs?

7. Safety pins are sold in boxes of 25. How many boxes can be filled from 840 safety pins?

8. A mini bus can carry 15 passengers. How many mini buses are needed to carry 98 people?

9. How many complete weeks are there in 160 days?

10. Atlases are packed in boxes of 20. How many boxes will be needed for the 250 atlases ordered by a school?

B

1. A river ferry can take 48 cars on each trip. How many crossings does the ferry need to make to carry 600 cars?

2. Felt tips are sold in packets of 12. How many packets can be made up from 152 felt tips?

3. Cans of drink cost 65p. How many cans can be bought with £10?

4. A school hall can fit 28 chairs into one row. How many rows are needed to seat 460 parents?

5. There are 25 milk cartons in each pack. A school needs 460 cartons. How many packs does it need to order?

6. A Rugby Union team has 15 players. How many teams can be made from 131 players?

7. A family saves £120 every month towards their £1000 holiday. How many months will it take to save the £1000?

8. How many 60 cm lengths of string can be cut from 65 metres?

9. Each egg box holds 6 eggs. How many boxes are needed for 350 eggs?

10. There are 16 sausages in each pack. How many packs can be made up from 500 sausages?

C

1. Each box contains 75 pills. How many boxes can be filled from 5000 pills?

2. One coach of a train can carry 72 passengers. How many coaches are needed to carry 1200 passengers?

3. There are 13 players in a Rugby League team. How many teams could you form from 205 players?

4. How many 350 g jars are needed to store 5 kg of marmalade?

5. A restaurant has 400 empty bottles. A crate holds 24 bottles. How many crates can be filled with empty bottles?

6. Amy walks to school every morning in order to save the 65p bus fare. How often does she need to do this before she has saved up the £30 she needs to buy a new pair of trainers?

7. A hot dog costs £1.20. How many hot dogs can be bought with £25?

8. Each coach can carry 53 passengers. How many coaches are needed to carry 3000 football supporters to an away match?

9. There are 960 staples in each box. How many boxes can be filled from one million staples?

10. An author writes 1800 words every day. How many days does it take her to write one million words?

On this page you will learn to use factors to multiply or divide.

Examples $28 \times 18 = 28 \times 6 \times 3 = 168 \times 3 = 504$

$576 \div 18 = (576 \div 3) \div 6 = 192 \div 6 = 32$

A

Copy and complete.

1. $14 \times 6 = 14 \times 3 \times 2 =$
2. $15 \times 8 = 15 \times 2 \times 2 \times 2 =$
3. $9 \times 12 = 9 \times 3 \times 2 \times 2 =$
4. $7 \times 15 = 7 \times 3 \times 5 =$
5. $14 \times 9 = 14 \times 3 \times 3 =$
6. $96 \div 12 = 96 \div 3 \div 2 \div 2 =$
7. $126 \div 9 = 126 \div 3 \div 3 =$
8. $156 \div 12 = 156 \div 3 \div 2 \div 2 =$
9. $180 \div 15 = 180 \div 3 \div 5 =$
10. $210 \div 14 = 210 \div 7 \div 2 =$

B

Use factors to work out:

1. 45×18
2. 17×27
3. 24×15
4. $320 \div 16$
5. $336 \div 24$
6. $273 \div 21$
7. 19×14
8. 35×24
9. 21×16
10. $324 \div 18$

C

Use factors to work out:

1. $12 \times 3{\cdot}6$
2. $16 \times 4{\cdot}5$
3. $1{\cdot}3 \times 56$
4. $32 \times 1{\cdot}5$
5. $1{\cdot}7 \times 48$
6. $18 \times 5{\cdot}5$
7. $36{\cdot}8 \div 16$
8. $48{\cdot}3 \div 21$
9. $3{\cdot}96 \div 18$
10. $33 \div 15$
11. $40{\cdot}8 \div 24$
12. $5{\cdot}85 \div 45$
13. $2{\cdot}3 \times 27$
14. $14 \times 1{\cdot}8$
15. $2{\cdot}4 \times 35$
16. $26 \times 2{\cdot}8$
17. $80 \div 25$
18. $896 \div 32$
19. $41{\cdot}6 \div 52$
20. $4{\cdot}86 \div 27$

Now you will learn to work out a times-table by adding.

Example

EIGHTS	8	16	24	32	40	48	56	64	72	80
TENS	10	20	30	40	50	60	70	80	90	100
EIGHTEENS	18	36	54	72	90	108	126	144	162	180

A

Copy and complete the table to work out the 15 times-table.

FIVES	TENS	FIFTEENS
5	10	15
10	20	30
15	30	
20	.	
25	.	
.	.	
.	.	
.	.	
.	.	
50	100	

B

Copy and continue the tables to ×10.

SEVENS	TENS	SEVENTEENS
7	10	17
14	20	34

3s	20s	23s
3	20	23
6	40	46

C

Copy and continue the tables to ×10.

6s	30s	36s
6	30	36
12	60	72

8s	40s	48s
8	40	48
16	80	96

On this page you will learn to multiply a number by 49, 51, 99 or 101.

Examples

$17 \times 51 = (17 \times 50) + (17 \times 1)$
$\qquad\quad = 850 + 17$
$\qquad\quad = 867$

$17 \times 99 = (17 \times 100) - (17 \times 1)$
$\qquad\quad = 1700 - 17$
$\qquad\quad = 1683$

A
Work out
1. 9×19
2. 11×19
3. 13×19
4. 8×21
5. 21×21
6. 14×21
7. 18×19
8. 12×19
9. 24×19
10. 17×21

B
Work out
1. 13×51
2. 16×51
3. 18×51
4. 12×49
5. 15×49
6. 19×49
7. 11×101
8. 15×101
9. 17×101
10. 14×99
11. 16×99
12. 19×99
13. 17×51
14. 23×51
15. 24×49
16. 18×49
17. 19×101
18. 26×101
19. 18×99
20. 22×99

C
Copy and complete.
1. $\square \div 41 = 12$
2. $\square \div 39 = 13$
3. $\square \div 61 = 11$
4. $\square \div 59 = 12$
5. $\square \div 41 = 15$
6. $\square \div 39 = 16$
7. $\square \div 61 = 16$
8. $\square \div 59 = 14$
9. $\square \div 41 = 17$
10. $\square \div 39 = 19$

Now you will learn to multiply by partitioning.

Examples

$79 \times 8 = (70 \times 8) + (9 \times 8)$
$\qquad\quad = 560 + 72$
$\qquad\quad = 632$

$5.3 \times 6 = (5 \times 6) + (0.3 \times 6)$
$\qquad\quad = 30 + 1.8$
$\qquad\quad = 31.8$

A
Work out
1. 36×4
2. 49×5
3. 38×6
4. 27×7
5. 44×8
6. 26×9
7. 43×4
8. 56×5
9. 62×6
10. 32×7

B
Work out
1. 72×6
2. 86×7
3. 59×8
4. 86×9
5. 73×7
6. 84×8
7. 7.5×6
8. 5.8×7
9. 9.2×8
10. 8.9×9
11. 6.7×6
12. 7.6×9
13. 83×6
14. 6.9×7
15. 75×8
16. 9.4×9
17. 96×6
18. 9.7×7
19. 68×8
20. 5.7×9

C
Copy and complete.
1. $\square \div 6 = 5.7$
2. $\square \div 7 = 8.3$
3. $\square \div 8 = 9.7$
4. $\square \div 9 = 6.9$
5. $\square \div 6 = 0.46$
6. $\square \div 7 = 7.8$
7. $\square \div 8 = 0.79$
8. $\square \div 9 = 8.7$
9. $\square \div 6 = 0.95$
10. $\square \div 7 = 0.67$

On this page you will practise multiplying a whole number or decimal fraction by any single-digit number.

Examples

$64 \times 7 = (60 \times 7) + (4 \times 7)$
$\qquad\quad = 420 + 28$
$\qquad\quad = 448$

$0.8 \times 3 = 2.4$

$1.6 \times 4 = (1.0 \times 4) + (0.6 \times 4)$
$\qquad\quad = 4 + 2.4$
$\qquad\quad = 6.4$

A

Write the answers only.

1. 16×2
2. 18×3
3. 26×2
4. 24×3
5. 27×4
6. 42×5
7. 23×6
8. 38×4
9. 14×7
10. 24×8
11. 38×5
12. 26×9
13. 0.3×2
14. 0.4×3
15. 0.5×7
16. 0.6×5
17. 0.4×6
18. 0.5×9
19. 0.8×5
20. 0.3×8
21. 0.7×4
22. 0.3×9
23. 0.5×6
24. 0.2×7

B

Copy and complete.

1. $58 \times 3 = \square$
2. $67 \times 4 = \square$
3. $0.4 \times 6 = \square$
4. $0.7 \times 8 = \square$
5. $3.6 \times 2 = \square$
6. $4.9 \times 5 = \square$
7. $5.3 \times 9 = \square$
8. $2.4 \times 7 = \square$
9. $64 \times \square = 128$
10. $0.7 \times \square = 3.5$
11. $4.7 \times \square = 14.1$
12. $2.4 \times \square = 19.2$
13. $39 \times \square = 156$
14. $0.9 \times \square = 6.3$
15. $2.3 \times \square = 13.8$
16. $3.5 \times \square = 28$
17. $\square \times 3 = 126$
18. $\square \times 5 = 230$
19. $\square \times 2 = 13.4$
20. $\square \times 4 = 3.2$
21. $\square \times 8 = 120$
22. $\square \times 7 = 14.7$
23. $\square \times 9 = 11.7$
24. $\square \times 6 = 5.4$

C

Copy and complete the tables.

1

×6	
63	→ 378
4·9	→
	→ 4·8
	→ 10·2
	→ 17·4
	→ 27·6

2

×7	
59	→
6·4	→
	→ 17·5
	→ 13·3
	→ 29·4
	→ 23·8

3

×8	
47	→
7·6	→
	→ 13·6
	→ 23·2
	→ 42·4
	→ 36·8

4

×9	
83	→
5·7	→
	→ 12·6
	→ 32·4
	→ 36·9
	→ 20·7

On this page you will practise:

- **multiplying a decimal fraction by 10 or 100.**

Examples $4 \cdot 58 \times 10 = 45 \cdot 8$ $6 \cdot 9 \times 100 = 690$

                  $3 \cdot 2 \times 10 = 32$ $0 \cdot 47 \times 100 = 47$

- **dividing a one or two-digit number by 10 or 100.**

Examples $65 \div 10 = 6 \cdot 5$ $4 \div 100 = 0 \cdot 04$

                  $7 \div 10 = 0 \cdot 7$ $23 \div 100 = 0 \cdot 23$

A

Multiply by 10.

1   3·4   **5**   12·3
2   1·36   **6**   0·5
3   0·03   **7**   2·08
4   4·8   **8**   7·3

Divide by 10.

9   2   **13**   5
10   12   **14**   48
11   6   **15**   34
12   25   **16**   9

Multiply by 100.

17   1·25   **21**   8·2
18   4·07   **22**   0·63
19   0·5   **23**   0·09
20   3·62   **24**   5·14

Divide by 100.

25   31   **29**   43
26   75   **30**   18
27   63   **31**   57
28   26   **32**   9

B

Work out

1   2·4 × 10   **9**   16 ÷ 10
2   1·37 × 100   **10**   6 ÷ 100
3   17·4 × 10   **11**   8 ÷ 10
4   8·2 × 100   **12**   39 ÷ 10
5   1·36 × 10   **13**   25 ÷ 100
6   0·5 × 10   **14**   1 ÷ 100
7   4·07 × 100   **15**   34 ÷ 100
8   0·63 × 100   **16**   86 ÷ 100

Copy and complete.

17   ☐ × 10 = 0·3
18   52 ÷ ☐ = 5·2
19   0·5 × ☐ = 50
20   ☐ ÷ 100 = 0·03
21   ☐ ÷ 10 = 0·7
22   ☐ × 100 = 9
23   2·08 × ☐ = 20·8
24   59 ÷ ☐ = 0·59
25   Ladybirds weigh 0·071 grams. How much do 100 ladybirds weigh?

C

Copy and complete the tables.

1

÷10
3 → 0·3
→ 1·7
→ 0·9
26 →

2

×100
4·71 → 471
13·9 →
→ 0·6
0·15 →

3

÷100
18 → 0·18
2 →
→ 0·05
36 →

4

×1000
→ 400
5·63 →
→ 2600
→ 8

5

÷1000
24 →
→ 0·006
→ 0·03
7 →

On this page you will practise:

- doubling a decimal fraction.

Examples　$0.67 \times 2 = (0.6 \times 2) + (0.07 \times 2)$　　$0.29 \times 2 = (0.2 \times 2) \times (0.09 \times 2)$
$$= 1.2 + 0.14 \qquad\qquad\qquad = 0.4 + 0.18$$
$$= 1.34 \qquad\qquad\qquad\qquad = 0.58$$

- halving a decimal fraction.

Examples　$0.27 \div 2 = (0.2 \div 2) + (0.07 \div 2)$　　$0.56 \div 2 = (0.5 \div 2) + (0.06 \div 2)$
$$= 0.1 + 0.035 \qquad\qquad\qquad = 0.25 + 0.03$$
$$= 0.135 \qquad\qquad\qquad\qquad = 0.28$$

A

Double these numbers.

1	0.4	**9**	0.24
2	0.7	**10**	0.35
3	0.5	**11**	0.64
4	0.2	**12**	0.81
5	0.9	**13**	0.8
6	0.6	**14**	0.43
7	0.82	**15**	0.75
8	0.31	**16**	0.92

Halve these numbers.

17	0.6	**25**	1.2
18	0.44	**26**	0.92
19	0.8	**27**	1.8
20	0.36	**28**	1.0
21	0.52	**29**	0.82
22	0.68	**30**	1.6
23	1.4	**31**	2.4
24	0.84	**32**	0.74

B

Write the answers only.

1	0.3×2	**7**	$0.7 \div 2$
2	0.8×2	**8**	$0.26 \div 2$
3	0.09×2	**9**	$0.38 \div 2$
4	0.26×2	**10**	$0.08 \div 2$
5	0.72×2	**11**	$0.9 \div 2$
6	0.65×2	**12**	$0.45 \div 2$

Copy and complete.

13 ☐ $\times 2 = 0.76$

14 ☐ $\div 2 = 0.25$

15 ☐ $\times 2 = 1.7$

16 ☐ $\div 2 = 0.77$

17 ☐ $\times 2 = 1.4$

18 ☐ $\div 2 = 0.9$

19 ☐ $\times 2 = 0.34$

20 ☐ $\div 2 = 0.65$

21 ☐ $\times 2 = 0.98$

22 ☐ $\div 2 = 0.59$

23 ☐ $\times 2 = 1.32$

24 ☐ $\div 2 = 0.96$

C

Copy and complete the tables.

1

Double	
0.29	→ 0.58
0.35	→
0.315	→
0.69	→
0.825	→
0.665	→
	→ 1.9
	→ 1.45
	→ 0.35
	→ 1.75
	→ 0.67

2

Halve	
0.35	→ 0.175
0.86	→
0.3	→
0.73	→
0.98	→
0.57	→
	→ 0.125
	→ 0.775
	→ 0.895
	→ 0.545
	→ 0.235

On this page you will practise doubling and halving and learn to use partitioning to double and halve.

Examples

Double 58 = $(50 \times 2) + (8 \times 2) = 100 + 16 = 116$

Double 0·76 = $(0·7 \times 2) + (0·06 \times 2) = 1·4 + 0·12 = 1·52$

Half of 358 = $(300 \div 2) + (50 \div 2) + (8 \div 2) = 150 + 25 + 4 = 179$

Half of 13·5 = $(13 \div 2) + (0·5 \div 2) = 6·5 + 0·25 = 6·75$

A

Double each number.

1	36	6	66
2	44	7	58
3	54	8	260
4	85	9	470
5	47	10	7500

Halve each number.

11	92	16	148
12	154	17	740
13	66	18	1380
14	116	19	12 600
15	172	20	14 800

Double by partitioning.

21	164	25	159
22	118	26	187
23	176	27	173
24	195	28	166

Halve by partitioning.

29	362	33	336
30	274	34	318
31	358	35	394
32	282	36	376

B

Write the answer only.

1	640×2	13	$920 \div 2$
2	580×2	14	$194 \div 2$
3	870×2	15	$1360 \div 2$
4	7300×2	16	$16\,400 \div 2$
5	4900×2	17	$15\,600 \div 2$
6	7600×2	18	$17\,800 \div 2$
7	$8·2 \times 2$	19	$12·8 \div 2$
8	$5·6 \times 2$	20	$18·1 \div 2$
9	$8·9 \times 2$	21	$15·7 \div 2$
10	$0·95 \times 2$	22	$1·46 \div 2$
11	$0·67 \times 2$	23	$1·23 \div 2$
12	$0·98 \times 2$	24	$17·9 \div 2$

Work out by partitioning.

25	274×2	34	$4·72 \div 2$
26	396×2	35	$2·56 \div 2$
27	277×2	36	$3·38 \div 2$
28	483×2	37	$36·4 \div 2$
29	238×2	38	$2·78 \div 2$
30	369×2	39	$5·16 \div 2$
31	445×2	40	$43·2 \div 2$
32	257×2	41	$3·68 \div 2$
33	379×2	42	$6·94 \div 2$

C

Copy and complete.

1	$\square \times 2 = 15\,800$
2	$\square \times 2 = 18\,300$
3	$\square \times 2 = 13\,700$
4	$\square \times 2 = 17\,400$
5	$\square \div 2 = 182$
6	$\square \div 2 = 168$
7	$\square \div 2 = 256$
8	$\square \div 2 = 1850$
9	$\square \times 2 = 17·4$
10	$\square \times 2 = 13·9$
11	$\square \times 2 = 17·5$
12	$\square \times 2 = 18·1$
13	$\square \div 2 = 1270$
14	$\square \div 2 = 2490$
15	$\square \div 2 = 24·3$
16	$\square \div 2 = 17·6$
17	$\square \times 2 = 1·17$
18	$\square \times 2 = 1·38$
19	$\square \times 2 = 1·59$
20	$\square \times 2 = 1·23$
21	$\square \div 2 = 23·7$
22	$\square \div 2 = 1·94$
23	$\square \div 2 = 1·88$
24	$\square \div 2 = 1·79$

On this page you will learn to use doubling or halving to solve calculations.

Examples

- MULTIPLICATION

  a) Find 13×14
  $$13 \times 14 = 13 \times 7 \times 2$$
  $$= 91 \times 2$$
  $$= 182$$

  b) Find 14×15
  $$14 \times 10 = 140$$
  $$140 \div 2 = \underline{70}$$
  $$14 \times 15 = \overline{210}$$

  c) Find 46×25
  $$46 \times 25 = 23 \times 50$$
  $$= 11 \cdot 5 \times 100$$
  $$= 1150$$

- FRACTIONS

  Find $\frac{1}{12}$ of 90
  $$\frac{1}{3} \text{ of } 90 = 30$$
  $$\frac{1}{6} \text{ of } 90 = 15$$
  $$\frac{1}{12} \text{ of } 90 = 7 \cdot 5$$

- MULTIPLES

  Some multiples of 22 can be worked out by doubling.
  $$1 \times 22 = 22$$
  $$2 \times 22 = 44$$
  $$4 \times 22 = 88$$
  $$8 \times 22 = 176$$
  $$16 \times 22 = 352$$

These multiples can be used to solve calculations.
$$23 \times 22 = (16 \times 22) + (8 \times 22) - (1 \times 22)$$
$$= 352 + 176 - 22$$
$$= 352 + 154$$
$$= 506$$

$$13 \times 22 = (8 \times 22) + (4 \times 22) + (1 \times 22)$$
$$= 176 + 88 + 22$$
$$= 176 + 110$$
$$= 286$$

A

1 Make the 16 times-table by doubling the 8 times-table.

8 times-table	16 times-table
8	16
16	
24	
32	
40	80
48	
56	
64	
72	
80	

Work out by doubling or halving.
Show the method used.

2 13×50

3 16×50

4 18×50

5 23×50

6 48×50

7 37×50

8 8×15

9 12×15

10 15×15

11 16×5

12 28×5

13 34×5

Work out by doubling.

14
$1 \times 12 = \square$
$2 \times 12 = \square$
$4 \times 12 = \square$
$8 \times 12 = \square$
$16 \times 12 = \square$

15
$1 \times 18 = \square$
$2 \times 18 = \square$
$4 \times 18 = \square$
$8 \times 18 = \square$
$16 \times 18 = \square$

Use halving to solve.

16
$\frac{1}{2}$ of $60 = \square$
$\frac{1}{4}$ of $60 = \square$
$\frac{1}{8}$ of $60 = \square$

17
$\frac{1}{3}$ of $30 = \square$
$\frac{1}{6}$ of $30 = \square$
$\frac{1}{12}$ of $30 = \square$

B

1 Make the 18 times-table by doubling the 9 times-table.

Work out by doubling or halving.
Show the method used.

2 14 × 17
3 18 × 28
4 16 × 19
5 19 × 15
6 26 × 15
7 33 × 15
8 29 × 25
9 35 × 25
10 47 × 25
11 16 × 75
12 18 × 55
13 22 × 45

Work out some multiples of 32 by doubling.
Use them to work out:

14 12 × 32
15 22 × 32
16 17 × 32
17 11 × 32
18 25 × 32
19 19 × 32

Copy and complete. Use halving to solve the second and third problems.

20 $\frac{1}{3}$ of 3
$\frac{1}{6}$ of 3
$\frac{1}{12}$ of 3

21 $\frac{1}{3}$ of 150
$\frac{1}{6}$ of 150
$\frac{1}{12}$ of 150

22 $\frac{1}{3}$ of 42
$\frac{1}{6}$ of 42
$\frac{1}{12}$ of 42

23 $\frac{1}{3}$ of 6000
$\frac{1}{6}$ of 6000
$\frac{1}{12}$ of 6000

24 $\frac{1}{3}$ of 18
$\frac{1}{6}$ of 18
$\frac{1}{12}$ of 18

25 $\frac{1}{3}$ of 90
$\frac{1}{6}$ of 90
$\frac{1}{12}$ of 90

Copy and complete.
Use halving to solve the second problem.

26 $\frac{1}{10}$ of 41
$\frac{1}{20}$ of 41

27 $\frac{1}{10}$ of 290
$\frac{1}{20}$ of 290

28 $\frac{1}{10}$ of 50
$\frac{1}{20}$ of 50

29 $\frac{1}{10}$ of 3
$\frac{1}{20}$ of 3

30 $\frac{1}{10}$ of 0·4
$\frac{1}{20}$ of 0·4

31 $\frac{1}{10}$ of 1·8
$\frac{1}{20}$ of 1·8

C

Work out by doubling or halving.
Show the method used.

1 3·1 × 18
2 0·43 × 16
3 2·3 × 14
4 1·7 × 15
5 15 × 6·3
6 8·7 × 15
7 3·9 × 25
8 5·7 × 25
9 0·46 × 25
10 19 × 3·5
11 24 × 4·5
12 72 × 35

Work out some multiples of 36.
Use them to work out.

13 9 × 36
14 26 × 36
15 15 × 36
16 21 × 36
17 13 × 36
18 28 × 36

Find one twelfth of each number by halving one third and halving again.

19 270
20 0·6
21 15
22 0·36
23 45
24 6·9
25 0·3
26 51

Find one twentieth of each number by halving one tenth.

27 0·3
28 39
29 0·08
30 7
31 2·9
32 0·5
33 61
34 1·3

35 Copy and complete these times tables.

12 times-table	24 times-table	48 times-table
12	24	48
24		
36		
48		
60		
72		
84		
96		
108		
120	240	480

On this page you will learn the grid method for multiplication.

Examples

2397 × 6

×	2000	300	90	7	
6	12000	1800	540	42	= 14382

356 × 24

×	300	50	6	
20	6000	1000	120	7120
4	1200	200	24	+1424
				8544

A

Copy and complete.

1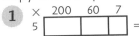

×	200	60	7	
5				=

2

×	100	40	5	
7				=

3

×	40	2
30		
9		=

4

×	60	3
20		
7		=

5

×	50	4
40		
8		=

6

×	80	5
20		
6		=

Use the grid method.

7 396 × 4

8 283 × 6

9 314 × 9

10 527 × 8

11 97 × 15

12 64 × 24

13 36 × 47

14 58 × 32

B

Copy and complete.

1

×	3000	700	50	2	
4					=

2

×	1000	300	60	4	
8					=

3

×	100	40	9	
20				
3				=

4

×	200	70	5	
40				
6				=

5

×	300	50	6	
30				
1				=

6

×	400	30	8	
50				
2				=

Use the grid method.

7 2950 × 7

8 2197 × 9

9 4583 × 6

10 4168 × 8

11 282 × 37

12 363 × 18

13 394 × 29

14 672 × 35

C

Copy and complete.

1

×	100	60	7	
50				
3				=

2

×	200	40	9	
20				
6				=

3

×	200	50	6	
100				
70				
4				=

4

×	400	20	8	
200				
90				
3				=

Use the grid method.

5 5263 × 7

6 6378 × 6

7 465 × 132

8 384 × 271

9 539 × 365

10 613 × 287

11 In one week 154 factory workers earn £347 each. What is the total wage bill?

On this page you will learn a standard method for short multiplication.

Examples

Method 1

```
                 4273
          ×         8
4000 × 8    32 000
 200 × 8     1600
  70 × 8      560
   3 × 8       24
            34 184
              1
```

Method 2

```
          4 2 7 3    Work from the right and carry.
    ×        8
          3 4 1 8 4
            2 5 2
```

A

Copy and complete.

1
```
              2389
       ×         5
2000 × 5
 300 × 5
  80 × 5
   9 × 5   ____
```

2
```
              2683
       ×         7
2000 × 7
 600 × 7
  80 × 7
   3 × 7   ____
```

3
```
              5476
       ×         8
5000 × 8
 400 × 8
  70 × 8
   6 × 8   ____
```

B

Use Method 1.

1
```
   3968
 ×    3
```

4
```
   1927
 ×    8
```

2
```
   4576
 ×    4
```

5
```
   4759
 ×    6
```

3
```
   3758
 ×    9
```

6
```
   2679
 ×    7
```

Use Method 2.

7
```
   2436
 ×    5
```

11
```
   3839
 ×    7
```

8
```
   2484
 ×    6
```

12
```
   3276
 ×    6
```

9
```
   1546
 ×    8
```

13
```
   2385
 ×    8
```

10
```
   2367
 ×    9
```

14
```
   4809
 ×    9
```

C

Use Method 2.

1 2763 × 6

2 3879 × 4

3 2729 × 9

4 1681 × 8

5 2675 × 7

6 4829 × 3

7 2736 × 7

8 3547 × 6

9 2974 × 9

10 3192 × 6

11 Each month an architect earns £2374. How much does he earn in 6 months?

12 The mean daily audience at a cinema is 1957. What is the total audience for the week?

On this page you will learn a standard method for the multiplication of decimals.

Examples

4.3×6

$4.0 \times 6 = 24.0$
$0.3 \times 6 = \underline{1.8}$
$\underline{25.8}$

2.57×4

$2.0 \times 4 = 8.0$
$0.5 \times 4 = 2.0$
$0.07 \times 4 = \underline{0.28}$
$\underline{10.28}$

3.692×7

$3.0 \times 7 = 21.0$
$0.6 \times 7 4.2$
$0.09 \times 7 0.63$
$0.002 \times 7 \underline{0.014}$
$\underline{25.844}$

Make sure that the decimal points are all in line.

A

Copy and complete.

1 8.6×2 $\quad 8.0 \times 2 = \square$
$ 0.6 \times 2 = \square$
$ \square$

2 3.4×8 $\quad 3.0 \times 8 = \square$
$ 0.4 \times 8 = \square$
$ \square$

3 2.3×6 $\quad 2.0 \times 6 = \square$
$ 0.3 \times 6 = \square$
$ \square$

4 6.9×5 $\quad 6.0 \times 5 = \square$
$ 0.9 \times 5 = \square$
$ \square$

5 3.5×9 $\quad 3.0 \times 9 = \square$
$ 0.5 \times 9 = \square$
$ \square$

6 4.2×7 $\quad 4.0 \times 7 = \square$
$ 0.2 \times 7 = \square$
$ \square$

7 A sprinkler uses 5·8 litres of water in one minute. How much water does it use in 4 minutes?

B

In each problem:
a) write down the multiplication.
   (Example: In Question 1 we have $\quad 4.96 \times 3$)
b) work out each bracket and find the total.

1 $(4.0 \times 3) + (0.9 \times 3) + (0.06 \times 3)$
2 $(3.0 \times 6) + (0.2 \times 6) + (0.04 \times 6)$
3 $(7.0 \times 8) + (0.2 \times 8) + (0.04 \times 8)$
4 $(6.0 \times 7) + (0.5 \times 7) + (0.02 \times 7)$
5 $(5.0 \times 9) + (0.3 \times 9) + (0.02 \times 9)$
6 $(8.0 \times 5) + (0.9 \times 5) + (0.07 \times 5)$
7 $(9.0 \times 4) + (0.4 \times 4) + (0.06 \times 4)$
8 $(3.0 \times 7) + (0.8 \times 7) + (0.05 \times 7)$

Set out as in the examples above.

9 2.48×7 $\qquad$ **15** 9.73×3
10 9.53×8 $\qquad$ **16** 3.95×7
11 3.78×4 $\qquad$ **17** 7.68×5
12 0.54×6 $\qquad$ **18** 6.59×9
13 5.47×9 $\qquad$ **19** 3.89×6
14 8.27×8 $\qquad$ **20** 6.58×8

21 One stone equals 6·35 kg. Niamh weighs 8 stones. How much does she weigh in kilograms?

C

1 3.163×6
2 0.247×5
3 5.938×3
4 5.723×9

5 8.362×7
6 4.671×8
7 2.945×4
8 7.283×9

9 4.874×7
10 9.284×8
11 6.754×6
12 7.456×9

13 2.31×16
14 3.54×24
15 4.67×32
16 2.95×52

17 5.34×45
18 3.78×34
19 8.57×27
20 4.86×63

On this page you will learn a standard method for long multiplication.

Examples

```
              46                          246
          ×   35                      ×    35
40 × 35    1400          200 × 35    7000
 6 × 35     210           40 × 35    1400
           1610            6 × 35     210
                                     8610
```

A

Copy and complete.

1
```
              41
          ×   13
41 × 10
41 × 3      ____
```

2
```
              51
          ×   23
51 × 20
51 × 3      ____
```

3
```
              32
          ×   13
32 × 10
32 × 3      ____
```

4
```
              25
          ×   15
25 × 10
25 × 5      ____
```

Work out

5 38 × 15   **8** 67 × 29

6 45 × 26   **9** 59 × 42

7 83 × 37   **10** 74 × 34

B

Copy and complete.

1
```
              163
          ×    16
163 × 10
163 × 6     ____
```

2
```
              381
          ×    25
381 × 20
381 × 5     ____
```

3
```
              258
          ×    38
258 × 30
258 × 8     ____
```

4
```
              429
          ×    43
429 × 40
429 × 3     ____
```

Work out

5 347 × 28   **8** 386 × 52

6 439 × 32   **9** 468 × 26

7 292 × 19   **10** 534 × 37

C

Copy and complete.

1
```
              217
          ×  124
217 × 100
217 × 20
217 × 4     ____
```

2
```
              531
          ×  245
531 × 200
531 × 40
531 × 5     ____
```

Work out

3 284 × 139   **7** 315 × 259

4 423 × 256   **8** 234 × 167

5 336 × 194   **9** 543 × 293

6 528 × 127   **10** 348 × 326

11 A book has 184 pages. The mean number of words per page is 317. How many words are there in the book?

12 A film company hires 426 extras to film crowd scenes. They are paid £275 each. What is the total wage bill?

On this page you will learn an informal method for division.

Examples

231 ÷ 6

Approximate 180 ÷ 6 = 30
240 ÷ 6 = 40
231 ÷ 6 lies between 30 and 40.

Calculate 231
           − 60   (10 × 6)
           171
          −120   (20 × 6)
           51
          − 48   (8 × 6)
            3

Answer 38 remainder 3

618 ÷ 22

618 ÷ 22 is approximately 600 ÷ 20 which is 30.

Calculate 618
          −220   (10 × 22)
           398
          −220   (10 × 22)
           178
          −110   (5 × 22)
            68
          − 66   (3 × 22)
            2

Answer 28 remainder 2

A

Work out

1 116 ÷ 5
2 110 ÷ 6
3 170 ÷ 7
4 199 ÷ 8

5 116 ÷ 9
6 238 ÷ 5
7 253 ÷ 8
8 261 ÷ 7

9 142 ÷ 6
10 193 ÷ 9
11 171 ÷ 4
12 212 ÷ 8

13 211 ÷ 6
14 306 ÷ 7
15 329 ÷ 5
16 320 ÷ 9

B

Work out

1 217 ÷ 14
2 660 ÷ 31
3 602 ÷ 24
4 686 ÷ 42

5 900 ÷ 37
6 841 ÷ 38
7 586 ÷ 13
8 640 ÷ 36

9 634 ÷ 51
10 970 ÷ 44
11 956 ÷ 27
12 746 ÷ 45

13 581 ÷ 22
14 830 ÷ 39
15 630 ÷ 26
16 999 ÷ 33

17 A tourist exchanges £46 for 598 Swedish kroner. How many kronor would £1 buy?

C

Work out

1 490 ÷ 23
2 567 ÷ 15
3 1176 ÷ 21
4 1000 ÷ 24
5 619 ÷ 18
6 830 ÷ 16

7 706 ÷ 32
8 1066 ÷ 26
9 1321 ÷ 43
10 774 ÷ 29
11 982 ÷ 37
12 1066 ÷ 19

13 There are 32 screws in each bag. How many bags can be filled from 1504 screws?

14 24 identical crates weigh 864 kg altogether. What is the weight of one crate?

15 Aaron earns £19 656 in a year. How much is he paid each week?

On this page you will learn a standard written method for division.

SHORT DIVISION

```
     32 R4
6 ) 196
 − 18      (3 × 6)
    16
 −  12     (2 × 6)
     4
```

LONG DIVISION

```
                   or              34
26 ) 884                    26 ) 884
 − 780    (30 × 26)          −  78     (3 × 26)
   104                         104
 − 104    (4 × 26)          − 104     (4 × 26)
     0                           0
Answer = 34
```

DIVISION OF DECIMALS

```
7 ) 87·5
 − 70·0   (10 × 7)
   17·5
 − 14·0   (2 × 7)
    3·5
 −  3·5   (0·5 × 7)
    0·0
Answer = 12·5
```

A

Set out as in the short division example above.

1. 257 ÷ 6
2. 268 ÷ 7
3. 206 ÷ 8
4. 553 ÷ 9

5. 228 ÷ 5
6. 385 ÷ 8
7. 381 ÷ 7
8. 234 ÷ 9

9. 437 ÷ 8
10. 855 ÷ 9
11. 201 ÷ 7
12. 664 ÷ 8

13. Eight sweets weigh 224 grams. What is the weight of one sweet?

14. A prize of £162 is shared by six winners. How much should each person receive?

B

Work out

1. 9) 423
7. 24) 912

2. 8) 375
8. 32) 928

3. 6) 327
9. 5) 66·5

4. 7) 483
10. 6) 128·4

5. 13) 351
11. 8) 210·4

6. 17) 578
12. 7) 224·7

13. An astronaut weighs 76·8 kilograms. On the Moon he weighs one sixth of his weight on Earth. How much does he weigh on the Moon?

C

Set out as in the examples.

1. 410 ÷ 19
9. 537·6 ÷ 8
2. 800 ÷ 28
10. 67·34 ÷ 7
3. 789 ÷ 36
11. 190·4 ÷ 14
4. 861 ÷ 26
12. 388·8 ÷ 16

5. 615 ÷ 47
13. 515·2 ÷ 23
6. 22·68 ÷ 7
14. 999·6 ÷ 21
7. 411·3 ÷ 9
15. 880·2 ÷ 27
8. 50·58 ÷ 6
16. 697·3 ÷ 19

17. A full bucket of water is poured into an empty fish tank seven times. The tank now has 57·96 litres of water. What is the capacity of the bucket?

18. Lloyd saves £35 each week. How long will it take him to save £840?

On these pages you will learn:

- to recognise a negative number output.

Example   4 − 6

Press   [C] [4] [−] [6] [=]   ⟶   −2

- to key in and interpret money calculations.

Example   £2·48 + 62p   Change 62p to £0·62

Press   [C] [2] [·] [4] [8] [+] [0] [·] [6] [2] [=]   ⟶   3·1   Answer = £3·10

- to carry out calculations involving more than one step.

Example   6 × (29 + 32)   Operation in brackets first.

Press   [C] [2] [9] [+] [3] [2] [=] [×] [6] [=]   ⟶   366

- to use the calculator's memory.

Example   (32 + 41) × (87 + 48)

Press   [MRC] [C] [3] [2] [+] [4] [1] [=] [M+] [C] [8] [7] [+] [4] [8] [=] [×]
[MRC] [=]   ⟶   9855

- to key in fractions and interpret the decimal answer displayed.

Example $\frac{2}{7}$ rounded to decimal places.

Press   [C] [2] [÷] [7] [=]   ⟶   0·2857142   Answer = 0·29, correct to 2 decimal places

Example $\frac{1}{3}$

Press   [C] [1] [÷] [3] [=]   ⟶   0·3333333

This is an example of a recurring decimal.

A

Use a calculator to work out the problems and interpret the display.

1 12 − 93

2 24 − 84

3 45 − 72

4 33 − 59

5 26 − 68

6 38 − 79

7 7·56 + 82p + 79p

8 £6·37 + 98p + 67p

9 £11·47 − 76p − 84p

10 £12·00 − 45p − 92p

11 £3·45 × 24

12 £2·35 × 38

13 £43·20 ÷ 16

14 £58·90 × 19

15 83·2 + (2·8 × 6)

16 5 × (11·5 − 6·97)

17 1·56 + (2·74 × 6)

18 8 × (6·4 − 3·9)

Arrange these fractions in order, smallest first.

19 $\frac{1}{3}$ $\frac{3}{8}$ $\frac{7}{20}$

20 $\frac{13}{25}$ $\frac{23}{40}$ $\frac{9}{16}$

21 $\frac{2}{5}$ $\frac{7}{18}$ $\frac{5}{12}$

B

Use a calculator to work out the problems and interpret the display.

1 2·7 − 6·2

2 3·6 − 8·3

3 1·2 − 7·54

4 4·5 − 5·93

5 3·14 − 9·75

6 5·32 − 11·4

7 (£2·76 + 69p) × 8

8 (£6·35 − 87p) × 5

9 (£4·36 − 68p) × 15

10 (£3·12 − 57p) × 4

11 (£36·44 + 76p) ÷ 8

12 (£77·83 + 57p) ÷ 16

13 (92 − 65) × (46 + 87)

14 (66 + 49) × (63 − 27)

15 (84 − 38) × (47 + 29)

16 (173 − 128) × (94 − 67)

17 (64 − 38) × (4·7 + 2·9)

18 (5·4 − 2·9) × (68 + 47)

Arrange these fractions in order, smallest first.

19 $\frac{2}{7}$ $\frac{3}{11}$ $\frac{7}{24}$ $\frac{4}{15}$

20 $\frac{3}{5}$ $\frac{2}{3}$ $\frac{4}{7}$ $\frac{5}{9}$

21 $\frac{17}{20}$ $\frac{5}{6}$ $\frac{13}{15}$ $\frac{21}{25}$

C

Use a calculator to solve these problems.

1 A policeman has £3648·20 in a savings account at the start of the year. He makes no withdrawals. His monthly salary of £1,524 is paid into the account. How much money is in the account at the end of the year?

2 Ian has £28·40 in his bank account. He buys 6 shirts costing £15·40 each. He pays with a cheque. By how much will he be overdrawn?

3 Write down the fractions which have these decimal equivalents.
[Hint: Try dividing by 3, 6, 7, 9 etc]

a) 0·1111111

b) 0·2222222

c) 0·7777777

d) 0·3333333

e) 0·1666666

f) 0·8333333

g) 0·1428571

h) 0·4285714

i) 0·8571428

j) 0·090909

k) 0·181818

l) 0·5454545

USING A CALCULATOR

On this page you will use a calculator to solve problems.

A

Copy and complete by writing the missing number in the box.

1 $1.68 + \square = 2.57$

2 $3.45 + \square = 5.63$

3 $\square + 1.43 = 4.39$

4 $\square + 0.78 = 2.11$

5 $3.21 - \square = 1.68$

6 $4.37 - \square = 0.94$

7 $\square - 1.57 = 2.24$

8 $\square - 3.86 = 4.49$

9 $2.97 + \square = 5.32$

10 $4.49 + \square = 5.16$

11 $\square - 3.75 = 0.68$

12 $\square - 1.83 = 6.47$

Find three consecutive numbers which add up to:

13 81

14 114

15 195

16 222

17 Find three quarters of 26.

18 Danielle earns £5.90 per hour. How much does she earn in a week in which she works for 42 hours?

B

Copy and complete by writing the missing number in the box.

1 $4.35 + \square = 6.24$

2 $\square + 1.47 = 3.31$

3 $8.39 - \square = 1.64$

4 $\square - 2.75 = 3.58$

5 $6.23 \times \square = 43.61$

6 $\square \times 9 = 22.77$

7 $26.08 \div \square = 3.26$

8 $\square \div 6 = 4.63$

Find two consecutive numbers with a product of:

9 306

11 1190

10 506

12 2256

13 The temperature is 4.7°C. It falls 8.65°C. What is the new temperature?

14 What is 28% of £335?

15

The programmes for a circus cost 65p. Programme sales raise £732.55. How many programmes are sold?

16 One pound equals 1.4 dollars. Phoebe has 304.15 dollars. How much is this in pounds and pence?

C

1 15,289 people visit a castle in July. £55,040.40 is raised by the sale of entrance tickets. What is the cost of each ticket?

2 The maximum temperature recorded in one year in London was 28.4°C. The range of the temperatures recorded was 37.6°C. What was the minimum temperature?

3 The mean weight of the children in a class is 38 kg. Their total weight is 1026 kg. How many children are there in the class?

4 74% of the electors voted for the winning candidate. 9100 people voted for the other candidates. How many people voted for the winning candidate?

5 A vertical mine shaft is 328 metres deep. The entrance to the shaft is 136 metres above sea level. How far below sea level is the bottom of the shelf?

On this page you will learn to write and use formulae.

Examples

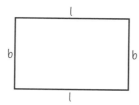

$p = 2l + 2b$, where p = perimeter

There are x people on a bus. One half of the passengers get off and 4 people get on. How many passengers (p) are on the bus?

$$p = \frac{x}{2} + 4$$

A

Find the perimeter (p) of each shape.

1

2

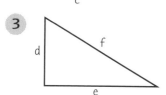

3

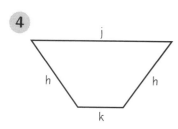

4

5

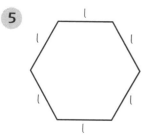

B

Draw and label the shape whose perimeter is given by each formula.

1 a triangle

$p = 3a$

2 an irregular pentagon

$p = 3b + 2c$

3 a quadrilateral

$p = 3d + e$

4 an irregular hexagon

$p = 3f + 2g + h$

5 Find the cost of:

a) 10 pens at x pence each

b) y sweets at 20 pence each.

6 A car has x litres of petrol in its tank. One half is used on Monday. A further 2 litres on Tuesday. How much petrol is left?

C

In the example above, the area (a) of the rectangle is given by the formula $a = lb$. (This means $l \times b$.)

1 Write a formula for the area (a) of the first three shapes in Section A.

2 Write a formula for the number of:

a) days (d) in w weeks.

b) months (m) in y years.

c) months (m) in d decades.

3 Write a formula for the nth term of each sequence.

a) 2, 4, 6, 8, 10

b) 3, 6, 9, 12, 15

c) −3, −2, −1, 0, 1

d) 1, 4, 9, 16, 25

e) 0·5, 1, 1·5, 2, 2·5

f) 1, 3, 5, 7, 9

On this page you will practise finding examples to match a general statement.

Examples

1. When you add two odd numbers, the answer is an even number.

   $5 + 11 = 16$ $7 + 3 = 10$

2. A multiple of 16 is also a multiple of 8.

   $48 = 3 \times 16$ and $48 = 6 \times 8$

 A

Find two examples that match these statements.

1. The sum of three consecutive numbers is three times the middle number.

2. To multiply a number by 50, multiply by 100 and halve the answer.

3. Dividing a number by 1 leaves the number unchanged.

4. Multiplying a decimal number by 100 moves every digit two places to the left.

5. The sum of the angles on a straight line is 180 degrees.

6. A multiple of 9 is also a multiple of 3.

7. The difference between two successive square numbers increases by two each time.

B

Find three examples that match these statements.

1. The sum of four consecutive numbers is double the sum of the middle pair of numbers.

2. To multiply a number by 25, multiply by 100 and divide the answer by 4.

3. Dividing a whole number by 0·5 makes the number twice as big.

4. Multiplying a decimal number by 1000 moves every digit three places to the left.

5. The sum of the angles in a triangle is 180 degrees.

6. A multiple of 12 is also a multiple of 6.

7. The difference between successive triangular numbers increases by one each time.

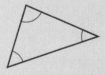

C

Find three examples that match these statements.

1. The sum of five consecutive numbers is five times the middle number.

2. To multiply a number by 15, multiply by 10, halve the answer and add the two parts.

3. Any square number is the sum of two consecutive triangular numbers.

4. Dividing a number by 0·1 makes the number ten times as big.

5. Dividing a number by 1000 moves every digit three places to the right.

6. The sum of the angles in a quadrilateral is 360 degrees.

7. A multiple of 18 is also a multiple of 3.

A

1	2		3	4	5
6		7		8	
	9		10		
11			12	13	
14	15			16	17
18			19		

Clues across

1. 4×19
3. 31×4
6. $167 + 41$
8. 6×7
9. $11 \cdot 6 \times 10$
12. $123 - 85$
14. $928 + 45$
16. $530 \div 10$
18. $2004 - 1989$
19. $401 - 299$

Clues down

1. 8×9
2. $542 + 59$
4. 6×4
5. 85×5
7. 9^2
10. 9×7
11. $224 - 33$
13. $8 \cdot 5 \times 100$
15. $300 \div 4$
17. $2 \times 2 \times 2 \times 2 \times 2$

B

Clues across

1. $413 - 61$
3. $0 \cdot 68 \times 100$
5. $3 \times 3 \times 3 \times 3$
6. 12^2
7. $980 \div 2$
8. $1003 - 985$
10. $472 + 256$
11. $712 - 618$
12. $4006 - 2994$

Clues down

1. $770 \div 2$
2. 17×3
3. 80×8
4. $173 - 89$
6. $0 \cdot 19 \times 100$
7. $5002 - 121$
8. $600 \div 5$
9. 9×49
10. $355 \div 5$

1	2			3	4
5			6		
		7			
	8				9
10				11	
12					

C

1	2	3		4	5
6			7		
8			9	10	
		11			
12	13			14	15
16				17	

Clues across

1. $311 - 92$
4. $275 \div 5$
6. $7001 - 347$
8. $0 \cdot 069 \times 1000$
9. 188×2
11. $422 - 53$
12. 21^2
14. $312 - 215$
16. 30×25
17. $1 \cdot 28 \times 50$

Clues down

1. 38×7
2. 13^2
3. $50 \times 1 \cdot 9$
5. $358 + 178$
7. $54 \cdot 5 \times 8$
10. $10\,003 - 2\,007$
11. $(366 + 254) \div 2$
12. $(9 \times 8) - 25$
13. $360 \div 8$
15. $0 \cdot 37 \times 200$

On these pages you will learn:

- **to choose the operation or operations needed to solve word problems.**

- **to decide whether the calculation will be done mentally or on paper.**

- **to use all four operations to solve the problems.**

Some of the problems require one operation only. Some require more than one.

a) Safraz has 128 books. Lucy has 96.
    How many do they have altogether?

    $128 + 96 = 224$
    They have 224 books altogether.

b) Maurice has 86 postcards.
    Libby has 55 more.
    How many do they have altogether?

    $86 + 55 = 141$
    $141 + 86 = 227$
    They have 227 postcards altogether.

- In each section read the problems and decide

a) what operations are needed.

b) whether the calculation will be done mentally or on paper.

Then solve the problems.

A

1 Abigail is driving 245 miles. She stops for petrol after 87 miles. How much further does she have to drive?

2 Connor buys a house for £93 500. When he sells it he makes a profit of £9000. What is the selling price?

3 Raoul is one eighth the age of his grandmother. His grandmother is 72. How old is Raoul?

4 Six racks of CDs each contained 18 CDs. How many CDs were there?

5 A cricket team scored 311 in the first innings of a match and 132 fewer in the second innings. How many did the team score in both innings?

6 How many hours are there in three weeks?

7 There were 143 skaters on an ice rink. During the next half hour 57 people started skating and 69 people stopped. How many skaters were there now on the rink?

8 One quarter of the 128 people on a school trip were adults.
   How many were children?

9 A greengrocer has seven boxes each containing 40 red apples. He also has five boxes of green apples. There are 400 apples altogether. How many green apples are there in each box?

10 36 children were asked what was their favourite day of the week. One third chose Saturday and one quarter chose Sunday. How many chose a weekday?

B

1. There were 216 people on the pier. 98 more people went on the pier while 63 left. How many were there now on the pier?

2. A large store had 288 skirts on display, equally divided between 18 rails. How many skirts were on each rail?

3. In June the average daily audience at a cinema was 240. How many people watched films at the cinema during the month?

4. The Matterhorn is 4428 m high. Owen is 939 m below the summit of the mountain. How high is Owen?

5. Niamh types at 60 words per minute. How long will it take her to type 3000 words?

6. Katharine won a race in a time of 13·86 seconds. Nicola was two tenths of a second slower. What was Nicola's time?

7. How many seconds are there in 12 hours?

8. An ice cream van has seven packets each containing 60 chocolate flakes. During the day 163 are used. How many flakes are left?

9. A display of flowers has three red flowers to every two white flowers. There are 32 white flowers. How many red flowers are there?

10. Of the 60 children in Year 6 two fifths had brown hair and three tenths had fair hair. How many of the children had hair of a different colour?

C

1. The River Nile is 6669 km long. The Yangtze-Kiang is 680 km shorter. How long is the Yangtze-Kiang?

2. The perimeter of a square playground is 120 m. What is the area of the playground?

3. Ashley won a race in 57·92 seconds. Adam was 48 hundredths of a second slower. Robert was seven tenths of a second behind Adam. What was Robert's time?

4. The average attendance at Arsenal's 25 away matches was 32 280. How many spectators watched Arsenal away from home that season?

5. In the Mars General Election the Independence Party polled 7 237 468 votes. 485 624 fewer Martians voted for the Inter Planetary Union Party. How many votes did the Inter Planetary Union Party poll?

6. How many hours are there in a leap year?

7. A sandwich bar makes 540 ham sandwiches every day. One packet of ham makes 15 sandwiches. How many packets does the sandwich bar need?

8. A theme park had 443 300 visitors in July. What was the average number of visitors per day?

9. Freda Frog had 50 tadpoles. All of Freda's children also had 50 tadpoles. All of Freda's grandchildren also had 50 tadpoles. How many great grandchildren does Freda have?

10. Two ninths of the 180 children in a school come by car. Five twelfths of the children walk. How many children travel to school in other ways?

On this page you will solve problems involving money.

DIXONS – PRICE LIST

Hi-Fi
£124

TV
£140

Personal Stereo
£35

Camera
£99

Roll of film
£4·20

Mouse Pad
£3·50

Printer
£85

Game Boy
£68

Alarm Clock
£14·99

Mobile Phone
£73

Audio Tapes
12 for £3·60

Batteries
6 for £4·50

Video Tapes
8 for £14

A

Work out the cost of each purchase and the change from £200.

1. a camera and 10 rolls of film
2. a hi-fi and 36 audio tapes
3. 2 mobile phones and 24 batteries
4. a TV and 16 video tapes
5. a printer and 3 mouse pads

6. Find the cost of:
   a) 1 video tape   b) 1 battery   c) 1 audio tape
7. How many rolls of film could be bought for £100?
8. How many hi-fis could be bought for £1000?
9. You buy a camera, an alarm clock and a computer game for £146·49. How much is the computer game?
10. You buy a mobile phone and one other item for £158. What is the other item?
11. In a sale all the prices are reduced by 10%. Find the cost of:
    a) the TV   c) the Gameboy
    b) the mouse pad   d) the camera

B

Find the value of these sales.

1. 3 cameras and 20 rolls of film

2. 2 hi-fis, a personal stereo and 18 batteries

3. A TV, a mobile phone and an alarm clock

4. 4 Game Boys, a printer and 4 mouse pads

5. 6 personal stereos, 2 cameras, an alarm clock and 60 audio tapes

6. Find the cost of:

   a) 3 video tapes   b) 5 batteries   c) 7 audio tapes.

7. Copy and complete the table by converting the pounds to the foreign currencies.

UK (pounds)	Europe (Euro)	Australia (dollar)	Canada (dollar)
£1·00	1·6	2·4	2·25
£10·00			
£15·00			
£50·00			

C

Find the value of these sales.

1. 5 cameras, an alarm clock and 100 rolls of film

2. 6 TVs, a personal stereo and 40 video tapes

3. 7 hi-fis and 96 audio tapes

4. 12 Game Boys, 4 alarm clocks and 16 mouse pads

5. 8 mobile phones, 4 printers and 90 batteries

6. How many rolls of film could you buy for £500?

7. How many personal stereos could be bought for £1000?

8. 3 TVs, 24 video tapes and a computer game are bought for £491. How much is the computer game?

9. Copy and complete the table by converting the pounds to the foreign currencies.

UK (pounds)	Brazil (real)	U.S.A. (dollar)	India (rupee)
£1·00	2·84	1·45	69·3
£10·00			
£25·00			
£500·00			

10. Using the table above, convert:

    a) 145 dollars into pounds   b) 69 300 rupees into dollars.

On these pages you will learn:

- **to use the relationship between metric units of length.**

10 mm = 1 cm	100 cm = 1 m
5 mm = 0·5 cm	50 cm = 0·5 m
1 mm = 0·1 cm	10 cm = 0·1 m
1 mm = 0·001 m	1 cm = 0·01 m

1000 m = 1 km
500 m = 0·5 km
100 m = 0·1 km
10 m = 0·01 km
1 m = 0·001 km

Examples

0·4 m = ☐ cm   Answer 40 cm

16 mm = ☐ m   Answer 0·016 m

4380 m = ☐ km   Answer 4·380 km

- **to suggest suitable units to measure lengths.**

If the length is less than 1 cm use millimetres.
If the length is less than 1 m use centimetres.
If the length is less than 1 km use metres.

We would use millimetres to measure the length of a ladybird.

A

Copy and complete by writing the missing number in the box.

1. 2000 m = ☐ km
2. 3500 m = ☐ km
3. 2·5 km = ☐ m
4. 7·400 km = ☐ m
5. 290 cm = ☐ m
6. 147 cm = ☐ m
7. 3·61 m = ☐ cm
8. 0·87 m = ☐ cm
9. 37 mm = ☐ cm
10. 16 mm = ☐ cm
11. 9 cm = ☐ mm
12. 0·4 cm = ☐ mm

Suggest a suitable metric unit to measure these lengths.

13. a charity walk
14. a necklace
15. a wood lice
16. the height of the classroom
17. a spoon
18. a cross-Channel swim

Think of three more things you would measure using:

19. millimetres
20. centimetres
21. metres
22. kilometres

Write the longest length from each pair.

23. 1·8 cm   8 mm
24. 0·2 cm   0·01 m
25. 6·23 m   623 mm
26. 90 m   0·1 km
27. 3·3 cm   50 mm
28. 370 m   0·04 km

B

Copy and complete.

1. 392 m = ☐ km
2. 2756 m = ☐ km
3. 1·437 km = ☐ m
4. 0·026 km = ☐ m
5. 240 cm = ☐ m
6. 6 cm = ☐ m
7. 0·48 m = ☐ cm
8. 13·96 m = ☐ cm
9. 21 mm = ☐ m
10. 685 mm = ☐ m
11. 0·007 m = ☐ mm
12. 6·937 m = ☐ mm

Suggest a suitable metric unit to measure these lengths.

13. a tic tac
14. the length of the River Amazon
15. a watch strap
16. the perimeter of a playground
17. a felt tip
18. a ski jump

Think of four more things you would measure using:

19. millimetres
20. centimetres
21. metres
22. kilometres

Copy and complete by putting >, < or = in the box.

23. 8417 mm ☐ 84·17 m
24. 23·1 cm ☐ 0·231 m
25. 7 m ☐ 0·007 km
26. 2460 cm ☐ 0·024 km
27. 5000 mm ☐ 0·05 km
28. 200 mm ☐ 0·02 m

C

Copy and complete the tables.

1.
mm	m
1650	→
9	→
→	4·218
→	0·014

2.
m	km
2700	→
3081	→
→	0·005
→	3·009

3.
cm	m
3	→
410	→
→	0·98
→	2·01

4.
cm	mm
	→ 20
0·7	→
→	0·3
→	17·5

Copy and complete each sentence by choosing the best estimate.

5. The height of Mount Everest is (0·89 km, 8·9 km, 0·089 km).
6. The thickness of an exercise book is (0·5 cm, 0·05 cm, 0·05 m).
7. A bed is (200 mm, 2000 mm, 20 000 mm) long.
8. The length of a pair of scissors is (0·13 m, 0·013 m, 13 mm).
9. A chair leg is (0·003 m, 0·03 m, 0·3 m) in length.
10. The length of a golf drive is (0·28 km, 0·028 km, 2·8 km).

Arrange these lengths in ascending order.

11. 5005 mm, 5·5 m, 555 cm, 0·005 km
12. 2700 m, 2·27 km, 0·772 km, 77 000 cm
13. 0·808 m, 888 mm, 88 cm, 0·008 km
14. 334 cm, 3·4 m, 0·033 km, 3334 mm

On this page you will learn to solve problems involving length.

A

1. Janice buys 8 shelves. Each shelf is 75 cm long. How many metres of shelving does this provide?

2. A square field has a perimeter of 3·6 km. What is the length of one side in metres?

3. Six equal lengths are cut from 2 m of string. 20 cm is left over. How long are the lengths of string?

4. Jonathan walks for 2·6 km. He rests and then walks a further 1400 m. How far does he walk altogether in kilometres?

5. At midday a shadow is 42 cm long. At 6 p.m. it is eight times longer. How long is the shadow at 6 p.m. in metres?

6. A mountain peak is 4·26 km above sea level. A climber is 549 m below the summit. How high above sea level is the climber?

B

1. George swims 4 km every day. The pool is 50 m in length. How many lengths does he swim in one week?

2. Seema cut 68 cm from 2 m of string. She then cut a further 35 cm. How much string is left?

3. A rectangular field is 1586 m long and 234 m wide. How long is the fence around it in kilometres?

4. A car travels 25 m every second. How far does it travel in kilometres in five minutes?

5. A carpenter needs sixteen 40 cm lengths of wood. How many metres of wood does he need to order?

6. In June a plant grew 1·5 metres. On average how much did it grow each day? Give your answer in millimetres.

C

1. A row of trees are 40 m apart. The row runs for 3 km. How many trees are there in the row?

2. The average width of Simon's paperback books is 16 mm. How many metres of shelving does he need to store his 275 books?

3. A garage entrance is 2·1 m wide. The car is 1·64 m wide. How many centimetres are there between each wall and the car?

4. An energetic slug slides 125 cm every hour. How long would it take the slug to travel one kilometre?

5. A roll of kitchen towels is 9·68 m long. Each towel is 22 cm long. How many towels are there in each roll?

6. A parachutist falls seven ninths of the distance to the ground before opening her parachute at 750 m above ground level. How high was the plane flying when she jumped?

On this page you will learn to read scales accurately.

For each of the scales work out
a) the measurement indicated by each of the arrows.
b) the difference between the two arrows.

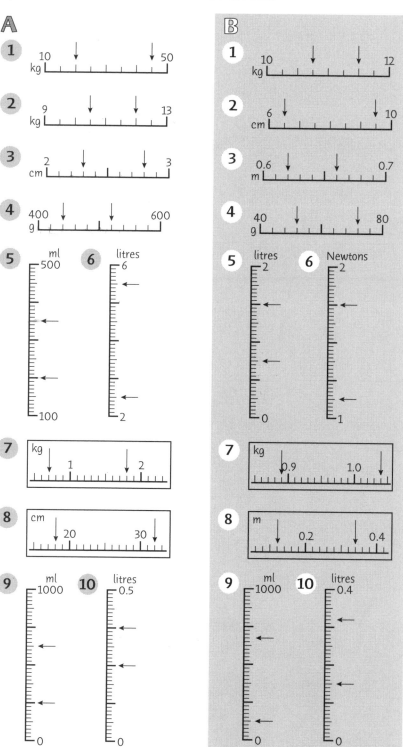

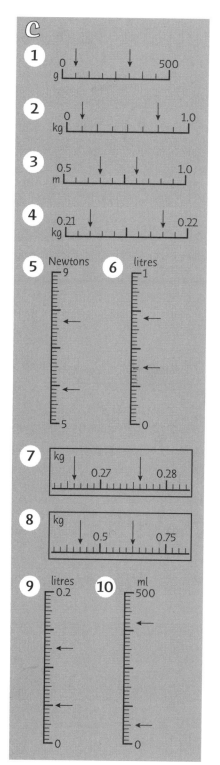

On this page you will learn to use the metric measures of mass, grams, kilograms and tonnes.

1000 g = 1 kg   1000 kg = 1 tonne (t)

A

Copy and complete by writing the missing number in the box.

1. 4 kg = ☐ g
2. 2·5 kg = ☐ g
3. 3·4 kg = ☐ g
4. 0·17 kg = ☐ g
5. 3100 g = ☐ kg
6. 2250 g = ☐ kg
7. 300 g = ☐ kg
8. 5740 g = ☐ kg
9. 1·75 kg = ☐ g
10. 5·92 kg = ☐ g
11. 8000 g = ☐ kg
12. 1600 g = ☐ kg

Write down which metric unit you would use to measure the mass of:

13. a bus
14. an ear ring
15. a jumbo jet
16. a slice of bread
17. a sack of coal
18. a teacher.

B

Copy and complete by writing the missing number in the box.

1. 1·3 kg = ☐ g
2. 4·25 kg = ☐ g
3. 6·148 kg = ☐ g
4. 3·7 kg = ☐ g
5. 1593 g = ☐ kg
6. 800 g = ☐ kg
7. 2760 g = ☐ kg
8. 25 g = ☐ kg
9. 2 t = ☐ kg
10. 1·64 t = ☐ kg
11. 1150 kg = ☐ t
12. 290 kg = ☐ t

Write down which metric unit you would use to measure the mass of:

13. a sparrow

14. a dining table
15. a bowl of fruit
16. an elephant
17. a lorry
18. a CD
19. a bed
20. a pear.

C

Copy and complete the tables.

1

g	kg
2486 →	
5 →	
120 →	
600 →	
→	3·475
→	0·025
→	1·84

2

kg	t
176 →	
1008 →	
17 →	
3200 →	
→	4·7
→	1·983
→	0·007

Copy and complete each sentence by choosing the best estimate.

3. A paperback book has a mass of about (0·001 kg, 0·01 kg, 0·1 kg).

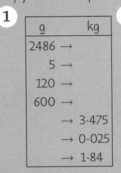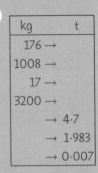

4. Many ice hockey players weigh about (0·1 t, 0·01 t, 0·001 t).

5. A radio cassette player weighs about (30 g, 300 g, 3000 g).

6. Marsha is 10. She has a mass of about (0·4 kg, 4 kg, 40 kg).

7. A shoe has a mass of about (0·03 kg, 0·3 kg, 3 kg).

8. A small car has a mass of about (1t, 10t, 100t).

On this page you will learn to solve problems involving weight.

A

1 The mean weight of the 12 apples in a bag is 150 g. What is the total weight of apples in kilograms?

2 Six identical eggs weigh 0·48 kg altogether. How much does each egg weigh in grams?

3 Samson lifts 0·31 t. Hercules lifts 43 kg less. How much does Hercules lift in kilograms?

4 An orange weighs 200 g. How much do 15 oranges weigh in kilograms?

5 A box of 50 chocolate bars weighs 10 kg. How much does each chocolate bar weigh in grams?

6 A bar of soap weighs 0·2 kg. 120 g are used. How much soap is left?

B

1 150 Oxo cubes weigh 0·9 kg. What does one Oxo cube weigh in grams?

2 Mrs. Gregg receives two parcels. One weighs 380 g. The other is twice as heavy. What is their combined weight in kilograms?

3 A loaf of bread weighs one kilogram. It contains 25 slices. What does each slice weigh in grams?

4 A shelf has 46 paperback books, each weighing 200 g. How much weight is the shelf supporting?

5 4 identical containers are loaded onto a lorry. Their combined weight is 2·74 t. What is the weight of each container in kilograms?

6 A ship has 4·2 tonnes of cargo in the hold. 1368 kg is removed. How much cargo is left?

C

1 The total weight of a rugby team is 1·35 t. What is the mean weight of the 15 players in the team?

2 A Weetabix weighs 25 g. A large box contains 72 biscuits. How much does the box weigh in kilograms?

3 A dinosaur was concerned about his weight of 52·4 tonnes. He began to work out at the Jurassic Gym. Three months later he had lost 2 763 kg. What did he weigh now?

4 A plane weighs 60·87 tonnes. 1 679 kg of cargo is loaded. How much does the plane weigh now?

5 Each tea bag contains 2·5 g of tea. How many tea bags can be made from 4 kg of tea?

6 The mean weight of the 196 passengers on a plane is 68 kg. What is their total weight in tonnes?

On this page you will learn to use the metric measures of capacity, litres, centilitres and millilitres.

$$10 \text{ ml} = 1 \text{ cl} \qquad 1000 \text{ ml} = 100 \text{ cl} = 1 \text{ litre}$$

A

Copy and complete by writing the missing number in the box.

1. 7 litres = ☐ ml
2. 3·681 litres = ☐ ml
3. 2·930 litres = ☐ ml
4. 0·500 litres = ☐ ml

5. 1800 ml = ☐ litres
6. 750 ml = ☐ litres
7. 3100 ml = ☐ litres
8. 600 ml = ☐ litres

9. 6·5 litres = ☐ ml
10. 1·8 litres = ☐ ml
11. 2250 ml = ☐ litres
12. 480 ml = ☐ litres

Write down which metric unit you would use to measure the capacity of:

13. a watering can

14. a beer barrel
15. a medicine bottle
16. a teardrop
17. a can of cola
18. a toilet cistern.

B

Copy and complete by writing the missing number in the box.

1. 1·25 litres = ☐ ml
2. 0·7 litres = ☐ ml
3. 4·58 litres = ☐ ml
4. 2·9 litres = ☐ ml

5. 1470 ml = ☐ litres
6. 680 ml = ☐ litres
7. 2300 ml = ☐ litres
8. 9070 ml = ☐ litres

9. 70 cl = ☐ litres
10. 0·5 litres = ☐ cl
11. 15 cl = ☐ ml
12. 200 ml = ☐ cl

Write down which metric unit you would use to measure the capacity of:

13. a syringe

14. an orange carton
15. a horse trough
16. a can of bicycle oil
17. an eyedrop
18. a jacuzzi
19. a sack of compost
20. a champagne bottle.

C

Copy and complete the table.

1.

ml	cl	litres
1284 →	→	
317 →	→	
6200 →	→	
5 →	→	
→	149 →	
→	70 →	
→	8 →	
→	200 →	
→	→	0·26
→	→	3·7
→	→	1·918
→	→	0·004

Copy and complete each sentence by choosing the best estimate.

2. An ink cartridge contains (2 cl, 20 cl, 200 cl) of ink.

3. A tablespoon has a capacity of (0·001 l, 0·01 l, 0·1 l).

4. A vase has a capacity of (6 ml, 60 ml, 600 ml).

5. A glass can hold (30 ml, 300 ml, 3000 ml) of drink.

6. A cereal bowl has a capacity of (45 cl, 450 cl, 4500 cl).

7. A bucket has a capacity of (0·05 l, 0·5 l, 5 l).

8. An ice cream scoop has a capacity of (8 ml, 8 cl, 8 l).

On this page you will learn to solve problems involving capacity.

A

1 A bottle of medicine contains 0·15 l. Paige takes 20 ml every day. How many bottles will she need in June?

2 A fish bowl contains 4·2 litres of water. 360 ml is spilt. How much water does the bowl hold now?

3 A sachet of shampoo contains 250 ml. There are twelve sachets in a box. How many litres of shampoo are there in the box?

4 A test tube holds 0·1 litres of a liquid. 38 ml is added. How much liquid is there in the test tube?

5 26 ml of cycle oil is used from a 200 ml can. A further 47 ml is used. How much oil is left?

6 How many 80 ml scoops of ice cream can be taken from a 2 litre tub?

B

1 Eight 350 ml beakers are filled from a full 4·5 litre flask of tea. How much tea is left in the flask?

2 A paddling pool contains 66·3 litres of water. 60 cl evaporates. How much water is left?

3 Darren fills a bath with 22·6 litres of hot water and 8·7 litres of cold water. He spills 4 cl getting in. How much water is left in the bath?

4 How many 20 cl cartons of milk can be filled from a 10 litre churn?

5 There are 12 bottles of wine in a box. Each bottle contains 70 cl. How much wine is there altogether in litres?

6 A petrol pump delivers 400 ml of petrol every second. How much petrol will it deliver in one minute?

C

1 A punch bowl contains 1·7 litres of drink. 70 cl of lemonade is added. The drink is shared among eight people. How much do they each have in millilitres?

2 A chemist makes 60 l of perfume. How many 150 ml bottles can be filled with the perfume?

3 A fireman's hose uses 80 cl of water every second. How many litres of water does it use in 5 minutes?

4 A horse trough holds 12·34 litres of water. Dobbin drinks 70 cl. Beauty drinks 875 ml. How much water is left?

5 A saucepan contains 1·6 l of boiling water. 137 ml evaporates before 25 cl is added. How much water is there now in the saucepan?

6 A bottle of soy sauce contains 150 ml. How much soy sauce is needed to fill 48 bottles. Give your answer in litres.

On this page you will learn to use the relationship between metric and imperial units.

THE METRIC MEASURES
The metric system of measures was invented in France in the C18th. All the units in the metric system are in tens, hundreds or thousands.

THE IMPERIAL SYSTEM
The imperial system of measures developed in Britain. Towards the end of the C20th it was officially replaced by the metric system, which is easier to use. However, many imperial measures are still in common use.

This table shows the most commonly used imperial units for length, mass and capacity, and their metric equivalents. (The sign "≈" means "is approximately equal to".)

LENGTH
1 inch ≈ 2·5 cm
1 foot ≈ 30 cm
1 yard ≈ 90 cm
1 mile ≈ 1·6 km
8 km ≈ 5 miles

MASS
1 ounce ≈ 30 g
1 kg ≈ 2·2 pounds

CAPACITY
1 pint ≈ 0·6 litres
1 gallon ≈ 4·5 litres

A

Copy and complete

1 2 inches ≈ ☐ cm
2 3 feet ≈ ☐ cm
3 5 ounces ≈ ☐ g
4 10 pints ≈ ☐ litres
5 2 gallons ≈ ☐ litres
6 10 miles ≈ ☐ km
7 2 yards ≈ ☐ cm
8 6·6 pounds ≈ ☐ kg
9 15 cm ≈ ☐ inches
10 45 litres ≈ ☐ gallons
11 40 km ≈ ☐ miles
12 9 m ≈ ☐ yards
13 10 kg ≈ ☐ pounds
14 1 m 50 cm ≈ ☐ feet
15 2·4 litres ≈ ☐ pints
16 240 g ≈ ☐ ounces

State which imperial unit your would use to measure the following.

Lengths
17 a motorway   19 a finger
18 a cricket pitch   20 a chair leg

Masses
21 eight apples   23 a bag of sugar
22 an egg   24 a CD

Capacities
25 a jug   27 a washing up bowl
26 a swimming pool   28 a bath

B

Copy and complete by putting > or < in the box.

1. 15 pounds ☐ 6 kg
2. 3 yards ☐ 3 m
3. 6 feet ☐ 1 m 90 cm
4. 6 miles ☐ 12 km
5. 8 ounces ☐ 225 g
6. 6 gallons ☐ 25 litres
7. 8 yards ☐ 7 m
8. 9 feet ☐ 2 m 60 cm
9. 12 pounds ☐ 5 kg
10. 9 gallons ☐ 42 litres
11. 12 ounces ☐ 370 g
12. 11 miles ☐ 20 km
13. 5 pints ☐ 2·5 litres
14. 4 inches ☐ 11 cm
15. 8 pints ☐ 4 litres
16. 100 yards ☐ 95 m

Copy and complete each sentence by choosing the best estimate.

17. A tin of beans has a mass of about (1 ounce, 11 ounces, 100 ounces).
18. A bed is about (4 feet, 6 feet, 8 feet) long.
19. A pen is about (6 inches, 9 inches, 12 inches) long.
20. The distance from London to Manchester is about (2 miles, 20 miles, 200 miles).
21. A can of cola holds about ($\frac{1}{2}$ pint, 2 pints, 12 pints).
22. A football pitch is about (1 yard, 10 yards, 100 yards) long.
23. An egg has a mass of about ($\frac{1}{2}$ ounce, 2 ounces, 12 ounces).
24. A car's petrol tank holds about (1 gallon, 10 gallons, 100 gallons).

C

Copy and complete by putting > or < in the box.

1. 9 miles ☐ 14 km
2. 17 ounces ☐ 0·5 kg
3. 7 yards ☐ 6·5 m
4. 8 gallons ☐ 35 litres
5. 11 inches ☐ 29 cm
6. 18 pounds ☐ 8 kg
7. 12 miles ☐ 20 km
8. 15 yards ☐ 14 m
9. 14 feet ☐ 4·1 m
10. 5 inches ☐ 12 cm
11. 4 pints ☐ 2·2 litres
12. 12 gallons ☐ 55 litres
13. 12 feet ☐ 3·5 m
14. 12 pints ☐ 7·5 litres
15. 27 ounces ☐ 0·8 kg
16. 80 miles ☐ 130 km

17. To the nearest litre, how many litres are there in:
    a) 2 gallons
    b) $2\frac{1}{2}$ gallons
    c) $1\frac{1}{2}$ gallons
    d) $3\frac{1}{2}$ gallons?

18. To the nearest tenth of a gallon, how many gallons are there in:
    a) 9 litres
    b) 5 litres
    c) 14 litres
    d) 18 litres?

19. To the nearest pound, how many pounds are there in:
    a) 100 kg
    b) 14 kg
    c) 5 kg
    d) 26 kg?

20. Rewrite the sentences in Section B, changing the chosen measurement to the approximate metric equivalent.

On these pages you will learn:

• to calculate the area and the perimeter of composite shapes that can be split into rectangles.

Example

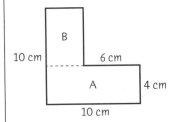

Area of whole shape = Area of A + Area of B
$$= (10 \times 4)\,cm^2 + (6 \times 4)\,cm^2$$
$$= 40\,cm^2 + 24\,cm^2 = 64\,cm^2$$

Perimeter $= 10\,cm + 10\,cm + 4\,cm + 6\,cm + 6\,cm + 4\,cm$
$$= 40\,cm$$

• to calculate the area of a right-angled triangle.

Example

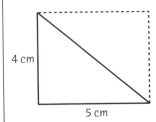

Think of the triangle as half of a rectangle.

Area of rectangle $= (5 \times 4)\,cm^2 = 20\,cm^2$
Area of triangle $= 20\,cm^2 \div 2 = 10\,cm^2$

A

Work out the perimeters of each of these shapes.

1 square   sides 12 cm

2 regular hexagon   sides 5 cm

3 regular octagon   sides 7 cm

4 equilateral triangle   sides 15 cm

5 Copy and complete this table showing the measurements of rectangles.

Length	9 cm	8 cm	6 cm	12 cm	6 cm	8 cm
Breadth	7 cm	3 cm				
Perimeter					26 cm	34 cm
Area			$12\,cm^2$	$60\,cm^2$		

6 A rectangular playground is 25 metres wide. It has an area of $1000\,m^2$.
How long is the playground?

7 Use $1\,cm^2$ squared paper. Draw three different rectangles each with an area of $36\,cm^2$.
Work out the perimeters.

8 Use $1\,cm^2$ squared paper. Draw three different rectangles each with a perimeter of 36 cm.
Work out the areas.

B

The length of these shapes are in cm. For each shape work out:

a) the area   b) the perimeter.

1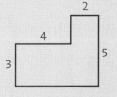

2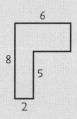

3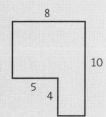

4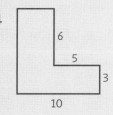

Use squared paper to draw the triangles.

For each triangle draw the other half of a rectangle.

Work out the area of: a) each rectangle   b) each triangle

5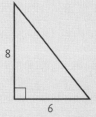

6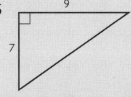

7

8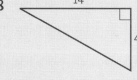

9 How many square millimetres are there in a square metre?

10 Use 1 cm² squared paper. Draw as many shapes with an area of 2 cm² as you can.

C

The lengths of these shapes are in cm. For each shape work out:

a) the area   b) the perimeter.

1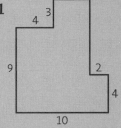

2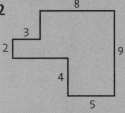

3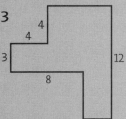

4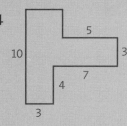

Work out the area of each triangle. All the lengths are in cm.

5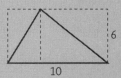

6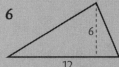

7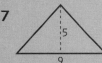

8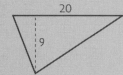

9 A room is 5 metres long by 3 metres wide. It costs £285 to carpet the room.
How much does the carpet cost per square metre?

10 Use 1 cm² squared paper. Draw as many shapes with an area of 3 cm² as you can.

On these pages you will learn to use the vocabulary related to time.

You should know and be able to use these facts and this rhyme.

1 millennium = 1000 years
1 century   = 100 years
1 year   = 12 months
             = 52 weeks
1 week   = 7 days
1 day   = 24 hours
1 hour   = 60 minutes
1 minute   = 60 seconds

'30 days has September,
April, June and November.
All the rest have 31,
Save for February alone,
Which has but 28 days clear
And 29 in each leap year.'

A

Write as

| minutes |

1 7 hours

2 $3\frac{3}{4}$ hours

3 360 seconds

4 75 seconds

| weeks |

5 6 years

6 21 days

7 140 days

8 20 years

| years |

9 60 months

10 13 weeks

11 19 decades

12 2 millennia

13 What will be the date two weeks after:
a) 24th June   b) 19th March   c) 27th May   d) 30th October?

Look at the calendar for August.
On what day of the week do these birthdays fall?

14 Andrea – August 8th

15 Joshua – August 19th

16 Vicky – July 26th

17 Tyrone – September 15th

AUGUST						
Su	M	Tu	W	Th	F	Sa
	1	2	3	4	5	6
7	8	9	10	11	12	13
14	15	16	17	18	19	20
21	22	23	24	25	26	27
28	29	30	31			

18 On what day of the week is the 1st of September?
Write out the calendar for September.

19 Gregory's birthday is three weeks after Christmas Day?
What is the date of his birthday?

20 March 1st is a Wednesday. How many Saturdays are there in April?

B

Write as

minutes		weeks		years

minutes

1. 14 hours
2. 2 days
3. 225 seconds
4. $\frac{1}{2}$ week

weeks

5. 11 years
6. 3 decades
7. 112 days
8. 840 hours

years

9. $37\frac{1}{2}$ decades
10. $3\frac{1}{4}$ millennia
11. 416 weeks
12. 66 months

13. What will be the date five weeks after:
   a) 6th May   b) 13th November   c) 28th June   d) 30th July?

Look at the calendar for December.
On what day of the week do these dates fall?

14. Epiphany – January 6th 2005
15. Remembrance Day – November 11th 2004
16. Hallowe'en – October 31st 2004
17. St. Valentine's Day – February 14th 2005
18. Write out the calendar for March 2005.

DECEMBER 2004						
Su	M	Tu	W	Th	F	Sa
			1	2	3	4
5	6	7	8	9	10	11
12	13	14	15	16	17	18
19	20	21	22	23	24	25
26	27	28	29	30	31	

C

1. Write *True* or *False* for each of the following statements.
   a) 40 years is longer than 15 000 days.
   b) There are less than 1000 hours in 6 weeks.
   c) Five hours is less than 20 000 seconds.
   d) One million minutes is more than two years.
   e) There are never enough minutes in a day.

2. What will be the date five weeks before:
   a) 12th March 2008   c) 6th June
   b) 24th October   d) 1st December?

Look at the calendar for April 2005.
On what day of the week do these dates fall?

3. St. Patrick's Day – March 17th
4. The longest day – June 21st
5. New Year's Day – January 1st, 2005
6. Christmas Day – December 25th
7. Write out the calendar for April 2006.

APRIL 2005						
Su	M	Tu	W	Th	F	Sa
					1	2
3	4	5	6	7	8	9
10	11	12	13	14	15	16
17	18	19	20	21	22	23
24	25	26	27	28	29	30

On this page you will learn to understand different times around the world.

Because the Earth rotates on its axis once every 24 hours, times are different around the world. The table shows the differences between the time in London (Greenwich Mean Time) and the times in other cities around the world.

City	Time Difference	City	Time Difference
Rome	+1	Jerusalem	+2
New York	−5	Buenos Aires	−3
Karachi	+5	Hong Kong	+8
Mexico City	−6	Los Angeles	−8
Tokyo	+9	Sydney	+10

A

What time is it in each of the cities in the table if it is 12·00 (noon) in London?

B

Write down the time in each of the cities in the table if the time in London is:
a) 04:00   b) 22:00.

C

1 An international company is based in London. It needs to contact its Head Offices in each of the cities in the above table when it is 09:00 in that city.
At what time would each telephone call need to be made from London?

2 Copy and complete the table showing arrival and departure times of international airline flights from London.

Depart	Flight (Hours)	Arrive	Local Time
16:00	2	Rome	
15:00	6	New York	
18:00	8	Karachi	
09:00	11	Mexico City	
17:00	13	Tokyo	
	4	Jerusalem	16:00
	13	Buenos Aires	15:00
	14	Hong Kong	10:00
	12	Los Angeles	18:00
	23	Sydney	08:00

On this page you will learn to solve problems involving time.

A

1 Reece started painting his room at 08:30. He finished at 15:10.
For how long was he painting?

2 A boat left Portsmouth at 14:40. It arrived at Cherbourg at 22:20.
How long did the voyage take?

3 The concert began at 19:45. It lasted for 2 hours 40 minutes.
At what time did it end?

4 An athlete began running a marathon at 10:15. He finished the race at 13:50.
For how long was he running?

5 Jason slept for eight and a half hours. He woke up at 07:10.
At what time did he go to sleep?

B

Lamb must be cooked for 30 minutes for every pound.
Write down how long the meat needs to be cooked if it weighs:

1 3 lb   **2** 2 lb   **3** 2·5 lb   **4** 5·5 lb.

5 Copy and complete the table showing cooking times for lamb.

Weight	Start	Finish
3 lb	11:00	
4·5 lb	15:30	
2·5 lb	12:50	
3·5 lb	16:40	

C

Chicken must be cooked for 20 minutes and then 40 minutes for every kilogram.
Write down how long a chicken needs to be cooked if it weighs:

1 2·5 kg   **2** 3·5 kg   **3** 1·25 kg   **4** 2·75 kg.

5 Copy and complete the table showing cooking times for chicken.

Weight	Start	Finish
1·5 kg	11:45	
2·25 kg	15:35	
1·75 kg		12:30
3·25 kg		18:30

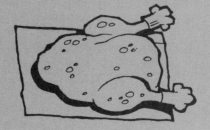

On these pages you will learn:

- **to recognise parallel and perpendicular lines.**

Parallel lines are lines that are the same distance apart for all their length. Railway lines are parallel lines.

Perpendicular lines cross or meet at right angles.

- **to recognise intersecting lines and intersections.**

Two lines that cross each other are called intersecting lines. The point at which they cross is an intersection.

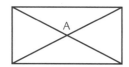

Point A is the intersection of the diagonals of the rectangle.

A

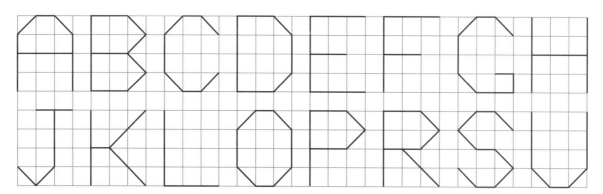

1. Use squared paper. Copy each of the letters above in a 3 × 4 grid. Show all the parallel lines with arrows or coloured pens or pencils, using a different colour for each pair of parallel lines in a letter. Show all the perpendicular lines by marking right angles.

2. Draw round a regular pentagon template (or trace the diagram). Draw on all the diagonals. How many intersections are there?

3. Investigate the diagonals of irregular pentagons. Do you always get the same number of intersections?

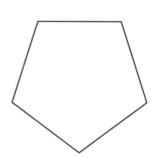

B

1 This quadrilateral has one pair of
parallel lines and two pairs of perpendicular lines.

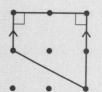

Use 3 × 3 grids on squared or dotty paper.
Find as many different quadrilaterals as you can.
Show all the parallel lines with arrows and show all the
perpendicular lines by marking a right angle.

2 Draw round a regular hexagon template (or trace the diagram).
Draw on all the diagonals. How many intersections are there?

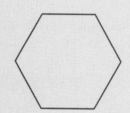

3 Investigate the diagonals of irregular hexagons.
Do you get the same result?

C

1 If you join 2 points to 2 points
you get one intersection.

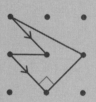

If you join 2 points to 3 points
you get three intersections.

Investigate joining 2 points to 2, 3, 4, 5, etc. points. Record your results in a table.
Use it to predict how many intersections you would get if you joined 2 points to 12 points.

2 This pentagon has been drawn in a 3 × 3 grid. It has one pair
of parallel lines and one pair of perpendicular lines.

Use 3 × 3 grids on squared or dotty paper.
Find as many different polygons with more than four sides as you can.
Identify all the parallel lines with arrows and show all the perpendicular
lines by marking a right angle.

Can you find shapes with:
a) 0   b) 1   c) 2   d) 3 pairs of parallel lines?

Can you find shapes with:
a) 0   b) 1   c) 2   d) 3   e) 4   f) 5   g) 6 perpendicular lines?

3 Copy the diagram.
   a) Draw a line through C which is perpendicular to AB.
   b) Draw a line through D which is perpendicular to AB.
   c) Draw a line through C which is parallel to AB.

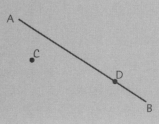

On these pages you will learn to classify 2-D shapes.

2-D shapes with straight lines are called *polygons*.
In the examples:

   equal lines are shown with dashes.

   equal angles are marked.

   parallel lines are shown with arrows.

A three sided polygon is a *triangle*.

scalene triangle

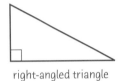
right-angled triangle

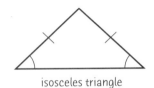
isosceles triangle

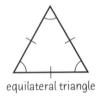
equilateral triangle

A four-sided polygon is a *quadrilateral*.

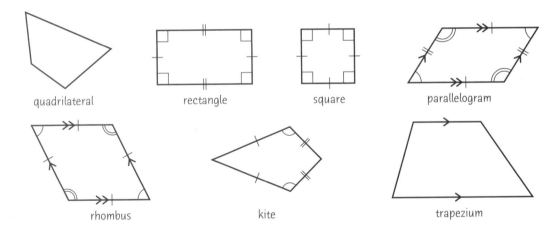

quadrilateral   rectangle   square   parallelogram

rhombus   kite   trapezium

OTHER POLYGONS   5 sides – pentagon   7 sides – heptagon
   6 sides – hexagon   8 sides – octagon

REGULAR POLYGONS

All sides and
all angles are equal.

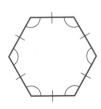

IRREGULAR POLYGONS

Sides and angles
are not all equal.

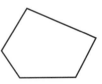

Here are some shapes.

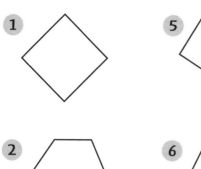
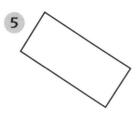
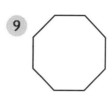
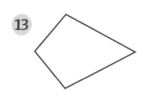
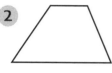

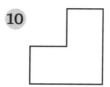
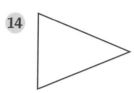

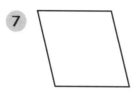
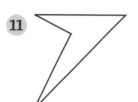
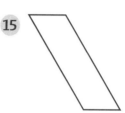
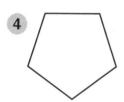
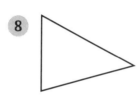

A

Write the name of each of the above shapes (e.g. irregular hexagon, trapezium, etc.).

B

Look at the quadrilaterals on page 92.
Write down which of the quadrilaterals have:

1 4 equal sides
2 2 equal sides
3 0 equal sides
4 equal opposite sides
5 equal adjacent sides
6 2 pairs of parallel lines
7 1 pair of parallel lines
8 no pairs of parallel lines
9 4 equal angles
10 2 equal angles
11 equal opposite angles
12 equal adjacent angles

C

Investigate the diagonals of the different types of quadrilateral shown on page 92.
State which of the quadrilaterals have:

1 diagonals that are equal.
2 diagonals that intersect (cross) at right angles.
3 diagonals that bisect one another (cut each other in half).

On these pages you will learn to use co-ordinates to find the position of a point beyond the first quadrant.

The position of a point on a grid is given by its x and y co-ordinates.

Examples

The position of point A.

x co-ordinate is −2.

y co-ordinate is 2.

Point A is (−2, 2).

Point B is (−3, −2).

Point C is (2, −1).

Point D is (1, 3).

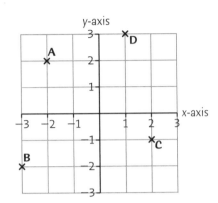

Remember: The x co-ordinate always comes first.

A

1. Use the grid to work out this word.
    (4, 5) (2, 2) (4, 4) (2, 1) (2, 1) (0, 1)

2. Use the grid to write the name of
    your school in co-ordinates.

3. Write your name in co-ordinates.

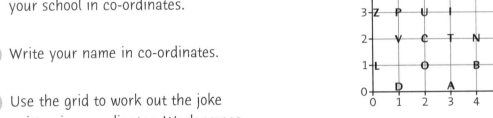

4. Use the grid to work out the joke
    written in co-ordinates. Work across.
    (0, 5) (4, 4) (5, 3) (3, 2)   (3, 3) (4, 5)
    (5, 4) (2, 5) (0, 1) (0, 1) (2, 1) (0, 5)   (5, 3) (4, 2) (1, 0)
    (5, 2) (2, 1) (2, 1) (1, 0)   (5, 3) (3, 2)   (5, 5) (5, 3) (3, 2) (4, 4) (4, 5)?

    (5, 3)   (4, 1) (5, 3) (4, 2) (5, 3) (4, 2) (5, 3)   (0, 5) (3, 3) (3, 2) (4, 4)
    (5, 3)   (2, 2) (5, 3) (0, 1) (2, 2) (2, 3) (0, 1) (5, 3) (3, 2) (2, 1) (5, 0).

5. Draw a 10 × 4 grid. (0–10 along the x-axis, 0–4 along the y-axis).
    Plot the co-ordinates and join them up in the order given to create a picture.

    (0, 3) (1, 3) (3, 4) (7, 3) (10, 4) (8, 2) (10, 0) (7, 1) (4, 0) (3, 0) (0, 1) (1, 2) (0, 3)

6. Use the grid above to write your own joke in co-ordinates.

B

1 Write down the co-ordinates of the letters.

2 Find the missing co-ordinates needed
   to complete these shapes.

   a) ABC and (☐, ☐) is a square.

   b) ADC and (☐, ☐) is a kite.

   c) CEF and (☐, ☐) is a rectangle.

   d) CDE and (☐, ☐) is a parallelogram.

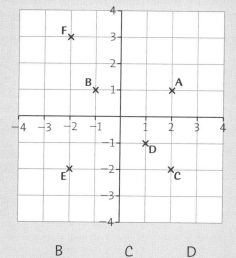

3 Draw a grid like the one above.
   Plot the points for shape A.
   Join them up in the order given.
   Use a different colour for each shape.
   Name the shapes.

A	B	C	D
(2,1)	(−3,−2)	(−4,−3)	(1,2)
(2,4)	(2,−2)	(−1,3)	(−2,2)
(−3,4)	(−2,1)	(2,−3)	(−2,−1)
(−3,1)	(−3,1)		(1,−1)

C

1 Use the grid to work out the joke written in co-ordinates.

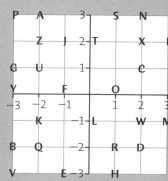

(2,−1) (1,−3) (−2,3) (0,2) (3,2) (1,3)

(−3,0) (−1,−3) (0,−1) (0,−1)(1,0) (2,−1) (−2,3) (2,3) (2,−2)

(−1,−3) (2,2) (0,2) (1,−2)(−1,−3) (3,−1) (−1,−3) (0,−1)(−3,0)

(2,−2) (−2,3) (2,3) (−3,1) (−1,−3) (1,−2) (1,0) (−2,1) (1,3)?

(1,3) (1,−3) (−2,3) (1,−2) (−2,−1)

(3,2) (2,3) (−1,0) (−1,−3) (1,3) (0,2) (−1,−3) (2,−2)

(2,1) (−2,1) (1,3) (0,2) (−2,3) (1,−2) (2,−2)

2 Write down the co-ordinates of the six letters in the
   second grid

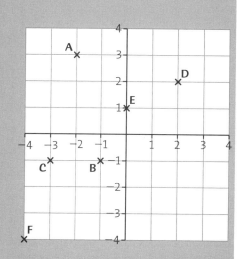

3 Find the missing co-ordinates to complete
   these shapes.

   a) ACD and (☐, ☐) is a square.

   b) FAD and (☐, ☐) is a kite.

   c) BED and (☐, ☐) is a rhombus.

   d) ADE and (☐, ☐) is a parallelogram.

   There are 3 possible answers to d).
   Can you find them all?

4 Use the grid in question 1 to write your own joke in co-ordinates.

On these pages you will learn to classify 3-D shapes according to their properties.

Some 3-D shapes with curved edges.

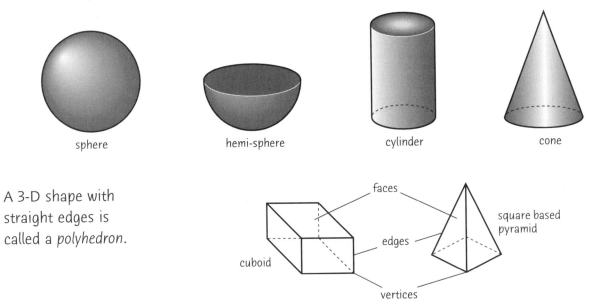

sphere   hemi-sphere   cylinder   cone

A 3-D shape with straight edges is called a *polyhedron*.

faces

square based pyramid

edges

cuboid

vertices

Regular polyhedra have faces which are identical.

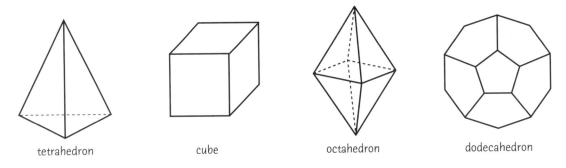

tetrahedron   cube   octahedron   dodecahedron

A *prism* is a polyhedron with two identical end faces and the same cross section throughout its length.

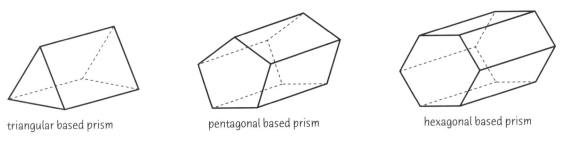

triangular based prism   pentagonal based prism   hexagonal based prism

Here are some shapes.

 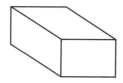 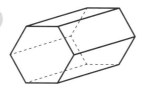 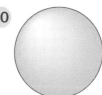

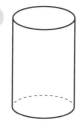 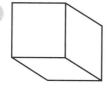 

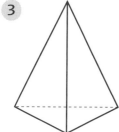 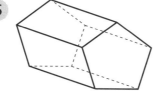 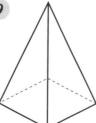 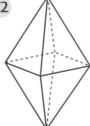

A

Copy and complete the table for each of the shapes.

No.	Shape	Faces	Edges	Vertices
1	cuboid	6	12	8

B

Describe the flat faces for each of the shapes.

Example

 1 The cuboid has 6 rectangles.

C

For each of the polyhedra and prisms above, write down:
a) the name of the shape.
b) the number of faces which have right angles.
c) the number of pairs of parallel faces.
d) whether any of the faces are perpendicular.
e) whether the number of edges meeting at each vertex is the same or different.

On this page you will investigate different ways of making polygons.

 A

Investigate the 2-D shapes you can make using a 3 × 3 grid on a pinboard or on squared or dotty paper. (A 3 × 3 grid has 4 small squares.)

How many different ways can you make a square, a parallelogram, a trapezium, etc?

Can you make symmetrical polygons?

What is the largest number of sides a shape can have?

B

Use a large square piece of card.

Mark the mid points of 3 sides

Draw these lines and then cut out the shapes.

Investigate the 2-D shapes you can make using different combinations of the card shapes.

How many different triangles, quadrilaterals, etc. can you make using all 6 pieces?

Can you make identical shapes using different combinations of some or all of the pieces?

Ask your own questions.

C

Use a large square piece of card.

Mark the mid points of each side.

Use the mid points to draw these lines. Cut out the shapes.

[The dotted lines are guide lines only.]

Investigate the different 2-D shapes you can make using different combinations of the card shapes.

Can you make a square with 2, 3, 4, 5, 6 pieces?

What shapes can you make using all the pieces?

Ask your own questions and investigate.

On this page you will learn to make nets for 3-D shapes.

A

1 Which of these nets will make a closed cube?

a)
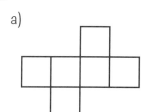

b)
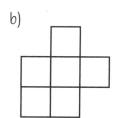

c)
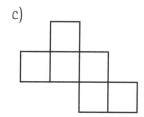

d)
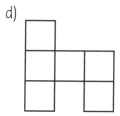

2 Copy the nets onto squared paper. Cut them out and see if you were right.

3 There are 11 different nets for a closed cube. Can you find them all?

B

1 Which of these nets will make a tetrahedron?

a)
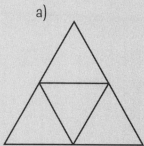

b)
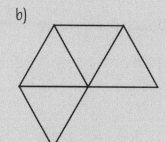

c)
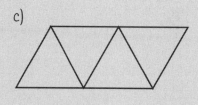

2 Copy the nets onto triangle dotty paper. Cut them out and see if you were right.

3 Use triangle dotty paper again.
Can you make a net for a triangular based prism?

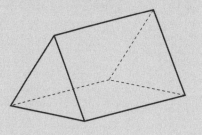

C

Use triangle dotty paper. Make nets for:

1 an octahedron

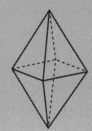

2 an hexagonal based prism.

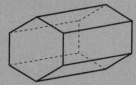

On this page you will learn to visualise 3-D shapes from 2-D drawings.

1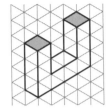

5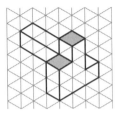

9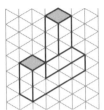

2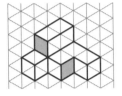

6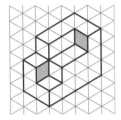

10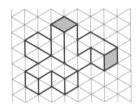

3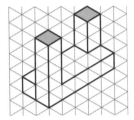

7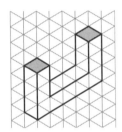

11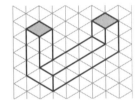

4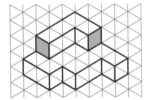

8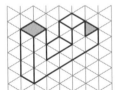

12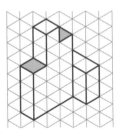

A

How many cubes are needed to build these shapes?

B

For shape 1 you need four cubes to cover and join the two shaded faces.
Work out how many cubes you need to cover and join the shaded faces in shapes 2 to 12.

C

1 Use triangle dotty paper. Copy the drawings.

2 Make 3-D shapes of your own using 5 cubes. Draw the shapes on triangle dotty paper.

On this page you will learn to sketch the pattern of a shape after it has been translated.

Translating a shape means moving it in a straight line.

Example

Translate the shaded shape:

1 left 6 squares (L6)

2 down 5 squares (D5)

3 left 5 squares, up 1 square (L5 U1)

4 left 2 squares, down 4 squares (L2, D4).

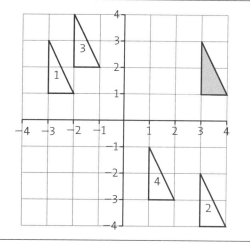

A

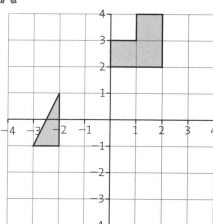

1 Copy the grid and the hexagon.
Translate the shape three times.
a) R2   b) L3   c) D3

2 Copy the grid and the triangle.
Translate the triangle three times.
a) U2   b) R4   c) L1

B

1 Copy the grid and the hexagon
in Section A.
Translate the shape three times.
a) L4 D2   b) L1 D3   c) R2 D1

2 Copy the grid and the triangle
in Section A.
Translate the triangle three times.
a) L1 U2   b) R3 D1   c) R4 U2

C

Plot the following triangles on grids like those above.
Sketch the positions after each of the translations.

1 (1, 1), (1, 3), (2, 1)
a) R2 D3
b) L3 U1
c) L4 D3

2 (−2, 1), (−1, 3), (0, 1)
a) R3 U1
b) L1 D4
c) R4 D3

3 (1, −1), (2, −2), (0, −3)
a) R1 U4
b) L3 D1
c) L2 U5

REFLECTIONS

On this page you will learn to sketch the reflection of a shape in a mirror line.

Examples

  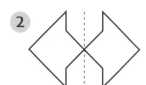

In each of the problems copy the shape and the mirror line and sketch the reflection.

A

1   2   3   4

B

1   3   5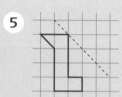

2 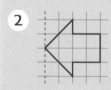   4 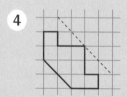   6

C

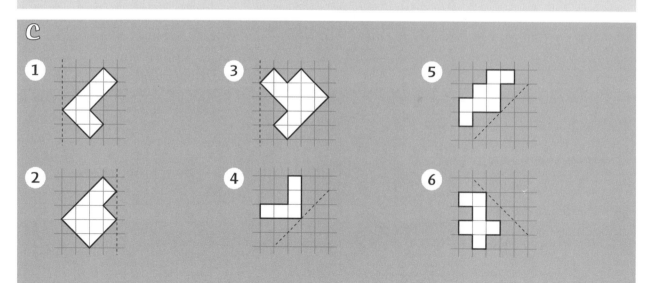

On this page you will learn to complete a symmetrical pattern and to sketch the reflection of a simple shape in two mirror lines.

Examples

Sketch the reflections of the shaded squares in both mirror lines.

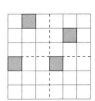 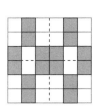 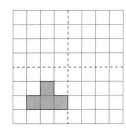 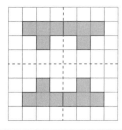

Copy each of the patterns onto squared paper. Shade in as many squares as necessary to complete the symmetrical patterns, as in the 6 × 6 grids above.

1 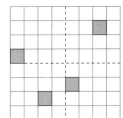   **2** 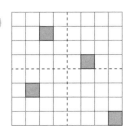   **3**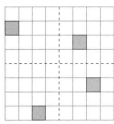

B

Copy each of the squares below onto squared paper.
Sketch the reflections of the shapes in both mirror lines.

1 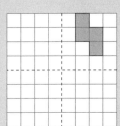   **2** 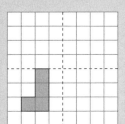   **3**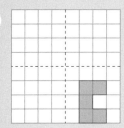

C

Copy each of the squares below onto squared paper.
Sketch the reflections of the shapes in both mirror lines.

1 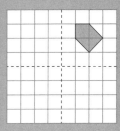   **2** 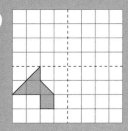   **3**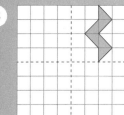

On this page you will learn to sketch the position of a shape after a rotation.

Example

A: 90° rotation about (0, 0)

B: 180° rotation about (0, 0)

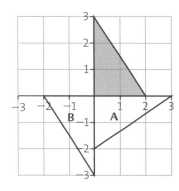

USEFUL TIPS

1 Imagine holding the point of rotation down with a pencil point.

2 90° rotation – horizontal lines become vertical and vice versa.

3 180° rotation – horizontal and vertical remain unchanged.

4 Use tracing paper.

Use squared paper. You can use tracing paper. For each of the following shapes:

a) copy the shape.
b) rotate the shape 90° about point A in a clockwise direction.
c) rotate the shape 180° about point A.

B

Copy the following shapes on grids showing all four quadrants, as in the example above. Rotate each shape both 90° and 180° about the origin, (0, 0), in a clockwise direction.

C

Join up the following points in the order given on grids showing all four quadrants, as in the example above. Rotate each shape about the origin, using the angle given.

1 (0, 0) (0, 3) (3, 1) (0, 0)   90° clockwise

2 (0, 0) (−2, 1) (−3, 3) (−1, 2) (0, 0)   180°

3 (0, 0) (−1, −2) (−3, −2) (−2, 0) (0, 0)   270° clockwise

4 (0, 0) (3, −3) (1, −3) (0, 0)   90° anticlockwise

On these pages you will learn to estimate, measure and draw angles accurately.

Angles measure the amount something turns or rotates. Angles are measured in degrees (°).

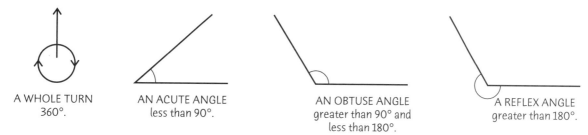

| A WHOLE TURN 360°. | AN ACUTE ANGLE less than 90°. | AN OBTUSE ANGLE greater than 90° and less than 180°. | A REFLEX ANGLE greater than 180°. |

USING A PROTRACTOR

A protractor is used to measure or draw angles accurately. Most protractors have two scales, a clockwise outer scale and an anti-clockwise inner scale. It is important to use the correct scale.

Examples

Outer Scale
$A\widehat{O}B = 50°$
$A\widehat{O}C = 140°$

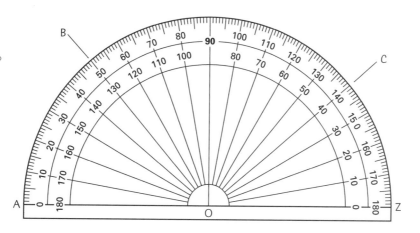

Inner Scale
$Z\widehat{O}C = 40°$
$Z\widehat{O}B = 130°$

360° protractors are easier to use when measuring reflex angles, but 180° protractors can be used to measure the inner angle made by the two lines, so that the reflex angle can be calculated. In the example of a reflex angle shown above, the inner angle is 120°. Therefore the reflex angle is 240°, because 360° − 120° = 240°.

COMMON MISTAKES

1. Using the wrong scale.
   Before measuring, decide if the angle is acute, obtuse or reflex. The angle in the example is 35° but could be read wrongly as 145°.

2. Reading the scale in the wrong direction.
   Make sure you look at the numbers on both sides of the line being measured. The angle in the example could be read wrongly as 45°.

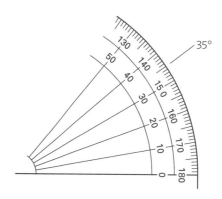

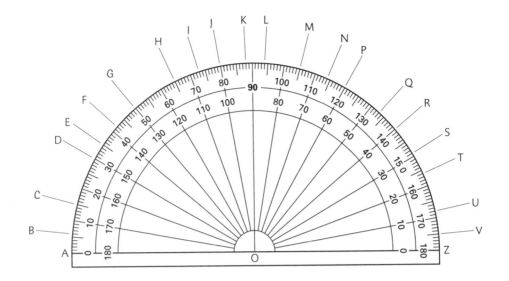

A

Use the above protractor.

Give the measurement of each angle.

1 AÔE   5 AÔH   9 ZÔR
2 AÔJ   6 AÔV   10 ZÔC
3 AÔR   7 ZÔM   11 ZÔP
4 AÔC   8 ZÔJ   12 ZÔE

Draw the following angles.

Label each angle acute or obtuse.

13 55°   15 15°   17 75°
14 140°   16 95°   18 155°

Measure these angles on the diagram on the opposite page.

19 AÔC   22 ZÔJ   25 AÔI
20 AÔK   23 ZÔF   26 ZÔM
21 AÔG   24 ZÔN   27 ZÔB

28 Measure these angles.

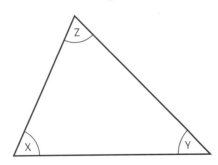

B

Use the above protractor.

Give the measurement of each angle.

1 AÔK   5 AÔD   9 AÔG
2 ZÔL   6 ZÔS   10 ZÔN
3 AÔU   7 AÔQ   11 AÔT
4 ZÔF   8 ZÔB   12 ZÔI

Draw the following angles.

Label each angle acute, obtuse or reflex.

13 62°   15 18°   17 240°
14 173°   16 91°   18 156°

Measure these angles on the diagram on the opposite page.

19 ZÔL   22 AÔD   25 ZÔH
20 AÔH   23 ZÔE   26 ZÔD
21 ZÔC   24 AÔB   27 AÔE

28 Measure these angles.

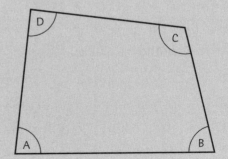

C

Give the measurement of these angles on the protractor on the opposite page.

1 AÔL **3** AÔF **5** ZÔU **7** AÔB **9** AÔM **11** AÔI

2 ZÔK **4** AÔS **6** ZÔQ **8** ZÔT **10** ZÔG **12** ZÔD

Draw the following angles. Label each angle acute, obtuse or reflex.

13 137° **14** 6° **15** 235° **16** 89° **17** 190° **18** 345°

Measure the following reflex angles.

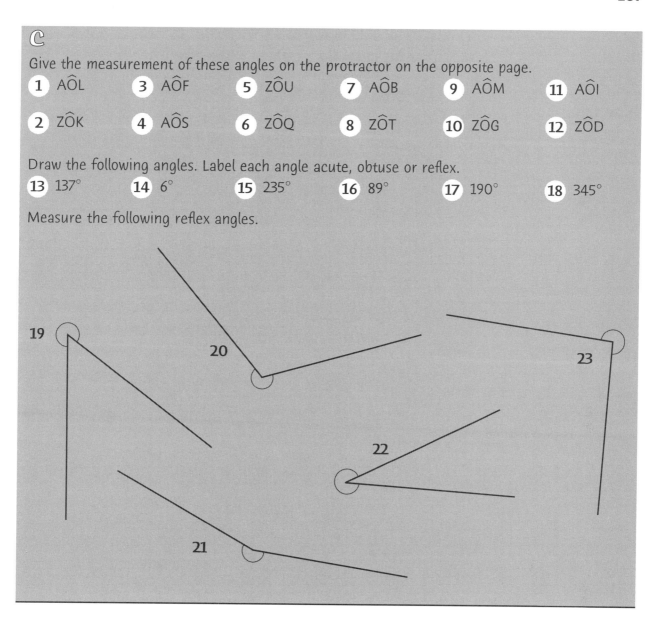

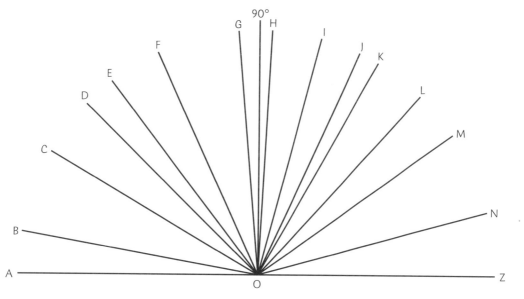

This diagram is used for questions 19 to 27 in Sections A and B on page 106.

On these pages you will learn to calculate angles on a straight line, at a point and in a triangle.

Examples

- ANGLES ON A STRAIGHT LINE
  The sum of the angles on a straight line is 180°.

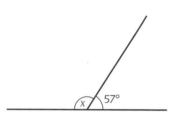

$$x + 57° = 180°$$
$$x = 123°$$

- ANGLES AT A POINT
  A whole turn is 360°.

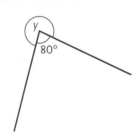

$$y + 80° = 360°$$
$$y = 280°$$

- ANGLES IN A TRIANGLE
  The sum of the angles in a triangle is 180°.

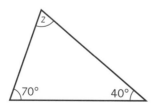

$$z + 110° = 180°$$
$$z = 70°$$

A

Find the angles marked with the letters.

1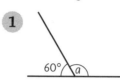

2

3

4

5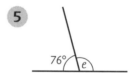

6

7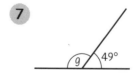

8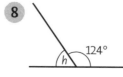

9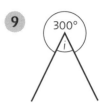

10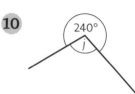

11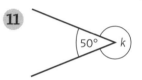

12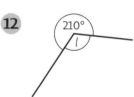

13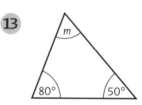

14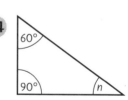

15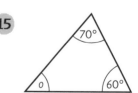

16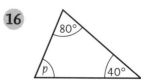

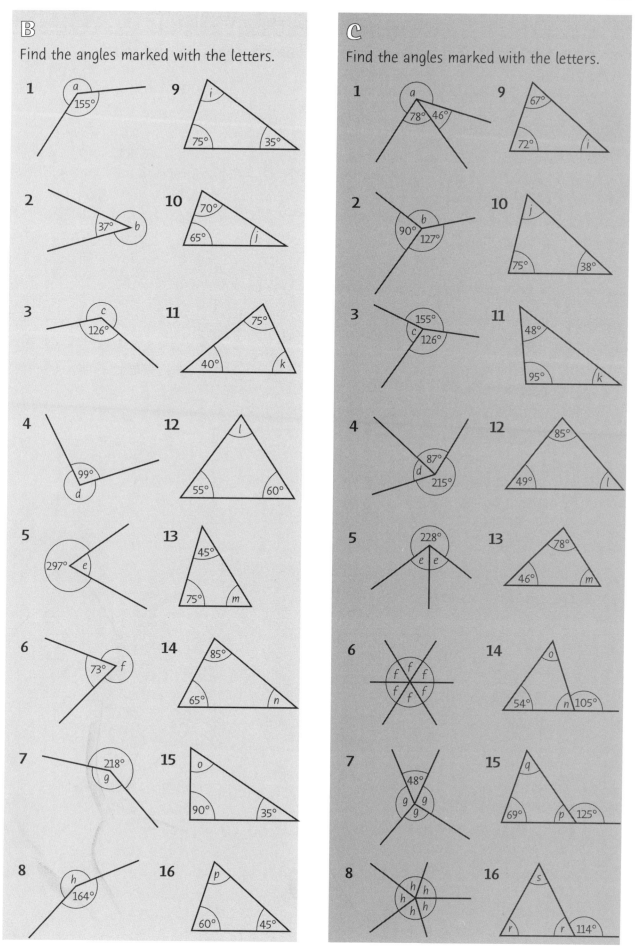

B

Find the angles marked with the letters.

1 a 155°
2 37° b
3 c 126°
4 99° d
5 297° e
6 73° f
7 218° g
8 h 164°
9 i 75° 35°
10 70° 65° j
11 75° 40° k
12 l 55° 60°
13 45° 75° m
14 85° 65° n
15 o 90° 35°
16 p 60° 45°

C

Find the angles marked with the letters.

1 a 78° 46°
2 b 90° 127°
3 155° c 126°
4 d 87° 215°
5 228° e e
6 f f f f
7 48° g g g
8 h h h h
9 67° 72° i
10 j 75° 38°
11 48° 95° k
12 85° 49° l
13 78° 46° m
14 o 54° n 105°
15 q 69° p 125°
16 s r r 114°

On these pages you will learn to use the language associated with probability.

The probability of something happening is the likelihood or chance that it might happen.

Examples

		PROBABILITY
1	The sun will rise tomorrow.	Certain
2	You will be younger next year.	Impossible
3	You spin a coin and get a tail.	Evens
4	You draw a card from a pack and get a heart.	1 out of 4
5	Tomorrow will be a sunny day.	?
6	Your teacher is a Martian.	?

The probabilities of these events can be placed on a scale. The first four statements could not be put anywhere else, but the last two depend upon the circumstances. You might choose to place them in these positions, especially if your teacher is rather odd.

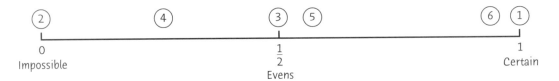

②	④	③ ⑤	⑥ ①

0
Impossible

$\frac{1}{2}$
Evens

1
Certain

 A

Place the probabilities of these events on a scale like the one above.

1 Christmas Day will be December 25th next year.

2 You will learn to drive when you grow up.

3 You have the same birthday as the Prime Minister.

4 The next child to join the school will be a girl.

6 The Queen has a cup of tea at breakfast.

7 The sun will rise in the west.

8 You will be invited to a party next month.

9 The next car to pass the school will be white.

10 Tomorrow will be a foggy day.

B

Work out these probabilities as a fraction and place each on a scale like the one on the opposite page.

1 Rolling a dice and not getting a 6.

2 Rolling a dice and getting a 0.

3 Rolling a dice and getting a number greater than 4.

4 Rolling a dice and getting a number less than 7.

5 Drawing a card from a pack and getting a club.

6 Drawing a card from a pack and getting a red card.

7 Drawing a card from a pack and not getting a spade.

8 Drawing a card from a pack and getting a king.

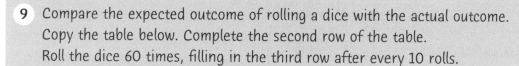

9 Compare the expected outcome of rolling a dice with the actual outcome.
Copy the table below. Complete the second row of the table.
Roll the dice 60 times, filling in the third row after every 10 rolls.

Number of rolls of dice	10	20	30	40	50	60
Number of odd numbers expected						
Actual number of odd numbers						

C

What is the probability of the arrow pointing at a shaded section when each of these spinners stops spinning?

Place each probability on a scale like the one on the opposite page..

9 Copy the table below. Complete the second row of the table.
Now roll a dice 60 times, filling in the third row every 12 rolls.

Number of rolls of dice	12	24	36	48	60
Number of 6s expected					
Actual number of 6s					

On this page you will learn to understand and use the terms range, mode, median and mean.

THE RANGE
The difference between the highest value and the lowest value.

THE MODE
The most common value.

THE MEDIAN
The middle value when the numbers are rearranged in order of size.

THE MEAN (OR AVERAGE)
The total divided by the number of items in the set.

Example
The marks achieved by 9 children in a test:
8 4 7 1 8 9 3 8 6

The range of marks is 8.
Highest − Lowest = 9 − 1
$$= 8$$

The mode is 8.
Eight occurs three times.

The median is 7.
1 3 4 6 (7) 8 8 8 9

The mean is 6.
Total marks ÷ no. of children = 54 ÷ 9
$$= 6$$

A

For each of the following sets of data find:
a) the range
b) the mode
c) the median.

1 The ages of five friends.
11 9 7 11 10

2 The goals scored by 11 footballers in one season.
0   2   1   0   1   7
   3   12   4   1   2

3 The daily maximum temperatures recorded in one week in March.

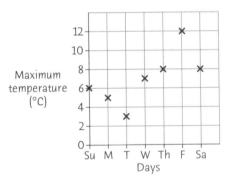

4 The daily hours of sunshine recorded in the same week.

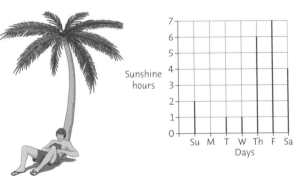

B

For each of the following sets of data find:
a) the range
c) the median
b) the mode
d) the mean.

1 The ages of 15 children at a birthday party.

2 5 7 3 4 3 6 2
3 5 6 4 5 2 3

2 The lengths in minutes of phone calls made by a bank manager.

3   2   8   4   3   12 5
7   15 3   10 2   4

3 The daily maximum temperatures recorded in one week in May.

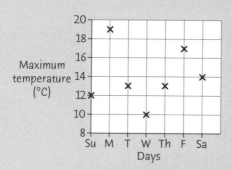

4 Joanne's marks in her weekly spelling test.

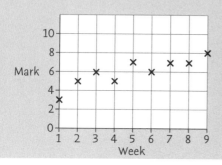

C

For each of the following sets of data find:
a) the range
c) the median
b) the mode
d) the mean.

1 The times in a 100 m sprint in seconds.

10·03   10·01   9·89   10·04   9·97
10·06   10·02   9·94   10·04

2 The heights jumped by 8 children.

1·00 m   0·96 m   1·05 m   0·74 m
1·04 m   1·12 m   0·89 m   0·96 m

3 Five people worked in an office.
The mean age of the people was 30 and the range of their ages was 6.

Write each sentence below and write next to it whether it is *Possible* or *Impossible*.
a) Every person was 30 years old.
b) All the people were at least 28 years old.
c) The oldest person was 35.
d) The youngest person was 26.

4 A teacher timed how long seven children took to complete a test.
The median time was 11 minutes and the range of times was 6 minutes.
Write each sentence below and write next to it whether it is Possible or Impossible.
a) The quickest time was 6 minutes.
b) The slowest time was 18 minutes.
c) The mean time was 8 minutes.
d) Three children took 12 minutes.

On these pages you will learn to draw and interpret bar charts with grouped data.

If the spread of a set of data is too large it is usually necessary to group the data before displaying it in the form of a graph.

Example

The ages of Mrs. Evans' family on the occasion of her 100th birthday party.

78	18	1	35	26	9
54	32	45	15	11	59
39	42	0	33	21	74
6	28	48	7	24	12
100	57	37	3	81	60

A tally chart showing the grouped ages.

Age	Tally	Frequency
0–19	⦀⦀ ⦀⦀	10
20–39	⦀⦀ ⦀⦀⦀⦀	9
40–59	⦀⦀ ⦀	6
60–79	⦀⦀⦀	3
80–99	⦀	1
100+	⦀	1
Total		30

The data in the tally chart can be displayed in a graph.

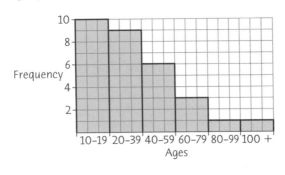

A

1 This bar chart shows the ages of children at a school disco.

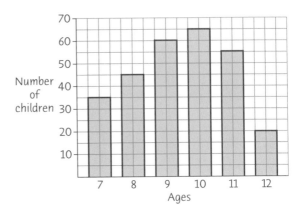

a) How many children were 9?
b) How many children were 11?
c) What was the age of the oldest child?
d) How many children were younger than 9?
e) How many children were older than 9?
f) How many children were there at the disco?

2 The distances achieved in a Welly Throwing Competition in metres.

19 24 37 22 18 29 42 14 10 26
31 16 23 30 36 8 27 11 32 24

Group the data in 10 metre intervals [0-9, 10-19 etc]
Make a tally chart and then display the data in a bar chart.

B

1 The children in one class took the following numbers of minutes to travel to school.

23 51   9 34 12 14 32 53 18 27
 7 29 17   3 43 36 11 25 42 15
24 46 10 16   9 13   8 22 31 14

Group the data in sets of 10 minutes. Make a tally chart and then display the data in a bar chart.

2 This graph shows the distance children in Year 6 travel to school.

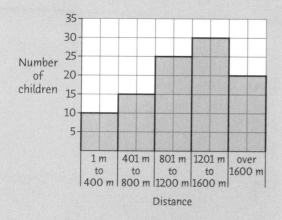

a) How many children live nearer to the School than 801 m?

b) How many children live further from the School than 800 m?

c) How many children are there in Year 6?

d) Anjali says that half the children in Year 6 travel more than 1200 metres to school.
Is she right? Explain your answer.

e) Copy and complete the sentence.
One in every ☐ children travels over 1600 metres.

C

1 The weights of the children in one Year 6 class in kilograms.

46 38 44 41 47 52 40 44 57 36
43 31 54 42 38 51 42 61 34 48
44 35 46 59 41 49 51 39 45 48

Group the data in sets of 5 kg.
Make a tally chart and then display the data in a bar chart.

2 This bar chart shows the percentage marks achieved by children in a Test.

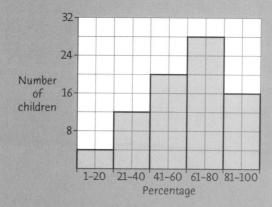

a) How many children scored below 41%?

b) How many children scored between 41% and 60%?

c) How many children scored more than 60%?

d) How many children took the test?

e) What proportion of the children scored over 80%.
Give your answer as a percentage.

f) The same children took the same test one term earlier. Draw a graph showing how you think the marks of that test would have been distributed.

On these pages you will learn to interpret pie charts.

Examples

The favourite colours of 80 children.

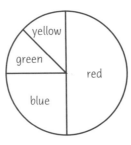

Colour	Children
red	40
blue	20
green	10
yellow	10

The 300 members of the audience at a performance of Toy Story.

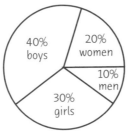

Group	Number
boys	120
girls	90
women	60
men	30

A

1

The pie chart shows the results of the 20 games played by a school football team.
How many games were:
a) won   b) lost   c) drawn?

2 The pie chart shows the 50 passengers travelling on a bus.
How many of the passengers were:

a) women   b) men   c) children?

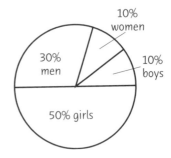

3

The pie chart shows the 60 competitors at an Athletics Meeting.
How many of the competitors were:
a) runners
b) jumpers
c) throwers?

B

1 The pie chart shows the 48 votes for the Year 6 candidates for the School Council. How many votes did each candidate receive?

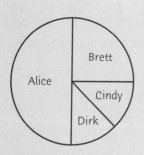

2

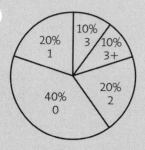

The pie chart shows the numbers of passengers in 200 cars.

Copy and complete the table.

Passengers	Cars
0	
1	
2	
3	
3+	

3 The pie chart shows the holiday destinations of 400 tourists waiting for their flights. How many tourists were travelling to each country?

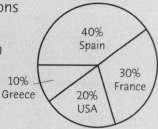

C

1

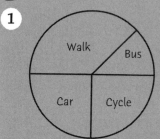

The pie chart shows how the children at one school travel to school each day.
70 children cycle. Estimate:
a) how many children travel by bus
b) how many children walk
c) how many children there are in the school.

2

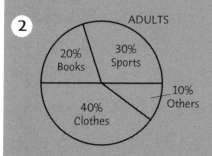

In a survey 60 adults and 80 children were asked to choose their favourite shop in a new shopping mall. The results are shown in the pie charts.

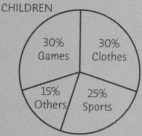

a) How many children chose games shops?
b) How many adults chose book shops?
c) Did more adults or children choose clothes shops?
d) Did more adults or children choose sports shops?

On this page you will learn to use a conversion graph.

Example

This graph converts miles into kilometres.

20 miles converts to 32 km.

64 km converts to 40 miles.

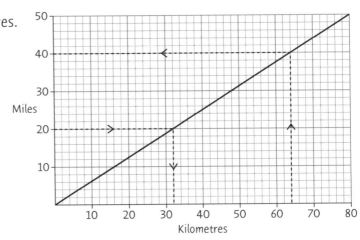

A

The rupee is the currency used in India.
This graph converts rupees into pounds.

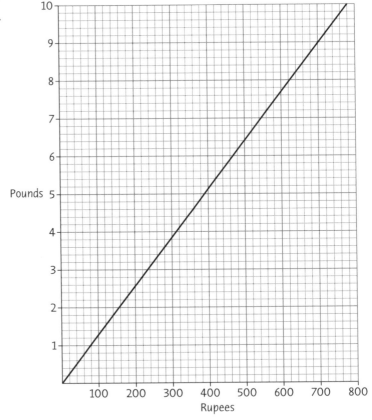

1 Convert into pounds:
   a) 280 rupees   d) 660 rupees
   b) 420 rupees   e) 380 rupees
   c) 600 rupees   f) 40 rupees.

2 Convert into rupees:
   a) £8·00   d) £7·40
   b) £4·60   e) £2·00
   c) £10·00   f) £6·60.

3 On holiday in India, Stanley bought
   snake charming lessons worth 9 pounds.
   How much did he pay in rupees?

B

This graph converts U.S. dollars to pounds.

1 Convert into pounds:
   a) 40 dollars
   b) 64 dollars
   c) 70 dollars
   d) 16 dollars
   e) 48 dollars
   f) 24 dollars.

2 Convert into dollars:
   a) £20
   b) £16
   c) £50
   d) £36
   e) £6
   f) £34.

3 Before flying home from New York the Wilson family bought gifts for 72 dollars.
   How much did they spend in pounds?

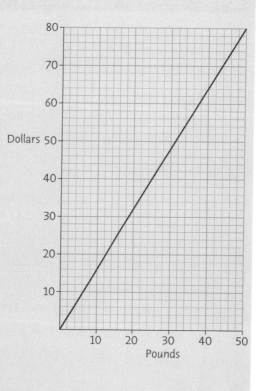

C

This graph converts kilograms to pounds.

1 Convert to the nearest tenth of a pound.
   a) 1 kg
   b) 1·9 kg
   c) 3 kg
   d) 0·9 kg
   e) 2·4 kg
   f) 0·5 kg

2 Convert to the nearest tenth of a kilogram.
   a) 4 lb
   b) 4·4 lb
   c) 1·3 lb
   d) 2·4 lb
   e) 4·6 lb
   f) 6·2 lb

3 Use graph paper to draw a graph converting test marks out of 60 to percentages.

Label the horizontal axis in 10s to 100.
Label the vertical axis in 10s to 60.
Join point (100, 60) to the origin (0, 0).

Use your graph to convert these marks to percentages.
   a) 30 out of 60
   b) 42 out of 60
   c) 57 out of 60
   d) 24 out of 60
   e) 51 out of 60
   f) 33 out of 60

Work out

1 1236 × 10

2 4·1 × 10

3 240 × 100

4 1597 × 100

5 528 × 1000

6 66 × 1000

7 18 750 ÷ 10

8 3·0 ÷ 10

9 43 700 ÷ 100

10 1 250 000 ÷ 100

11 85 000 ÷ 1000

12 4 630 000 ÷ 1000

Round to the nearest 10.

13 136   **15** 7245

14 874   **16** 1498

Round to the nearest 100.

17 8648   **19** 17 635

18 26 971   **20** 64 253

Round to the nearest 1000.

21 16 379   **23** 8542

22 127 600   **24** 59 837

Approximate by rounding to the nearest whole one.

25 14·6 + 8·3

26 25·5 − 17·8

27 8·6 × 4·1

28 53·7 ÷ 5·9

Estimate the numbers shown by the arrows.

29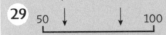
50 ↓   ↓ 100

30 0 ↓   ↓ 1

31 −5 ↓   ↓ 0

32 50 ↓   ↓70

33 −20 ↓   ↓ 0

34 0↓   ↓ 2

35 Copy and complete the table showing changes in temperature.

OLD	CHANGE	NEW
4°C	−10°C	
−7°C	+15°C	
−2°C		6°C
	−14°C	−3°C
−1°C	−8°C	
5°C		−11°C
	+9°C	4°C
−18°C	+13°C	
−13°C		3°C
	−17°C	12°C

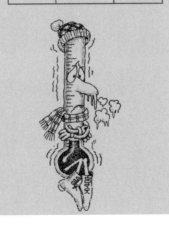

Copy each sequence and write the next four terms.

36 2·5 2·2 1·9 1·6

37 −20 −16 −12 −8

38 79 68 57 46

39 0·02 0·04 0·06 0·08

40 −14 −11 −8 −5

41 10 20 40 70

42 0·35 0·48 0·61 0·74

43 100 81 64 49

Find three numbers that are multiples of both:

44 6 and 7   **46** 5 and 8

45 4 and 13   **47** 3 and 25.

Write down the first prime number after:

48 8   **52** 44

49 14   **53** 55

50 20   **54** 80

51 32   **55** 90.

Find all the prime factors of:

56 27   **59** 76

57 66   **60** 90

58 45   **61** 84.

Work out

62 $8^2 + 5^2$ **65** 30^2

63 $9^2 − 7^2$ **66** 11^2

64 $10^2 + 6^2$ **67** 25^2

Copy and complete these equivalent fractions.

1 $\dfrac{3}{4} = \dfrac{\square}{20}$ **4** $\dfrac{3}{10} = \dfrac{21}{\square}$

2 $\dfrac{2}{5} = \dfrac{\square}{30}$ **5** $\dfrac{5}{6} = \dfrac{15}{\square}$

3 $\dfrac{7}{9} = \dfrac{\square}{18}$ **6** $\dfrac{7}{8} = \dfrac{35}{\square}$

Cancel each fraction into its simplest form.

7 $\dfrac{33}{55}$ **9** $\dfrac{32}{48}$

8 $\dfrac{80}{100}$ **10** $\dfrac{18}{42}$

Arrange in ascending order.

11 $\dfrac{5}{8}, \dfrac{3}{4}, \dfrac{1}{2}, \dfrac{9}{16}$

12 $\dfrac{5}{12}, \dfrac{1}{3}, \dfrac{1}{2}, \dfrac{5}{9}$

Change to mixed numbers.

13 $\dfrac{14}{5}$ **16** $\dfrac{14}{3}$

14 $\dfrac{27}{8}$ **17** $\dfrac{319}{100}$

15 $\dfrac{57}{10}$ **18** $\dfrac{60}{9}$

Change to improper fractions.

19 $8\dfrac{9}{10}$ **21** $6\dfrac{7}{11}$

20 $3\dfrac{5}{6}$ **22** $2\dfrac{17}{25}$

Write the fraction shaded in its simplest form.

23

24

Write as decimals.

25 $4\dfrac{32}{100}$ **27** $\dfrac{86}{1000}$

26 $1\dfrac{723}{1000}$ **28** $2\dfrac{9}{100}$

Write as mixed numbers.

29 5·35   **31** 6·127

30 23·04   **32** 2·008

Write the value of the underlined digit.

33 7·2<u>5</u>   **37** 2·47<u>9</u>

34 0·80<u>1</u>   **38** 48·<u>6</u>2

35 1<u>7</u>·08   **39** 0·10<u>5</u>

36 5·7<u>3</u>6   **40** 12·9<u>4</u>

41 Copy the line and locate the numbers.

1·05 1·08 1·025 1·065

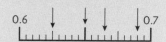

1.0   1.1

42 Write the number shown by each arrow.

0.6   0.7

Round to the nearest:
whole one   tenth.

43 3·74   **47** 4·61

44 4·29   **48** 29·38

45 29·81   **49** 3·45

46 106·52   **50** 37·83

51 Write in ascending order.

7·58, 0·78, 0·708, 7·08

52 Copy and complete the table.

Fraction	Decimal	%
$\dfrac{1}{10}$	0·1	10%
$\dfrac{37}{100}$		
$\dfrac{3}{4}$		
	0·72	
	0·3	
	0·09	
		50%
		23%
		7%

Find

53 $\dfrac{3}{8}$ of 40

54 $\dfrac{4}{5}$ of 60

55 $\dfrac{23}{100}$ of 3 m

56 $\dfrac{375}{1000}$ of 1 m

57 10% of 58

58 30% of 240

59 20% of £14·00

60 5% of £6·20

61 Lenny has 3 green marbles to every 4 red marbles. If he has 20 red marbles, how many green marbles does he have?

62 8000 people visited a castle. 70% were adults. How many were children?

Copy and complete.

1 $305 + 298 = \square$

2 $4 \cdot 8 + 3 \cdot 1 = \square$

3 $5 \cdot 7 + \square = 9 \cdot 5$

4 $3 \cdot 64 + \square = 4$

5 $\square + 6700 = 14\,300$

6 $\square + 0 \cdot 37 = 0 \cdot 87$

7 $4003 - 1986 = \square$

8 $8 \cdot 6 - 1 \cdot 9 = \square$

9 $4300 - \square = 1900$

10 $7 \cdot 1 - \square = 2 \cdot 8$

11 $\square - 0 \cdot 16 = 0 \cdot 6$

12 $\square - 5800 = 3700$

Work out

13   3249
    $+1563$

17   4753
    -1278

14   4385
    $+3948$

18   7480
    -2916

15   5167
    $+1856$

19   9619
    -5834

16   6478
    $+2757$

20   6250
    -5791

Set out correctly and find the totals.

21 $1 \cdot 25 + 14 \cdot 6$

22 $0 \cdot 309 + 8 \cdot 4$

23 $4 \cdot 31 + 17 \cdot 2 + 0 \cdot 695$

24 $25 \cdot 91 + 0 \cdot 8 + 1 \cdot 357$

Set out correctly and find the differences.

25 7186 and 15 470

26 729 and 42 031

27 $5 \cdot 31 - 1 \cdot 9$

28 $3 \cdot 2 - 1 \cdot 85$

Copy and complete

29 $7 \times 0 \cdot 6 = \square$

30 $15 \times 99 = \square$

31 $8 \times \square = 4 \cdot 0$

32 $1 \cdot 3 \times \square = 1 \cdot 3$

33 $\square \times 100 = 30$

34 $\square \times 7 = 4 \cdot 9$

35 $27 \div 10 = \square$

36 $0 \cdot 3 \div 2 = \square$

37 $12 \div \square = 0 \cdot 6$

38 $300 \div \square = 60$

39 $\square \div 6 = 1 \cdot 4$

40 $\square \div 100 = 3 \cdot 7$

Copy and complete.

41   1576
    $\times \quad 4$

43   4629
    $\times \quad 6$

42   2938
    $\times \quad 7$

44   3574
    $\times \quad 8$

Copy and complete.

45 $6\overline{)457}$

47 $5\overline{)83 \cdot 5}$

46 $14\overline{)314}$

48 $9\overline{)312 \cdot 3}$

Copy and complete.

49   325
    $\times \quad 19$

50   276
    $\times \quad 47$

Work out

51 $2 \cdot 38 \times 3$

53 $4 \cdot 72 \times 7$

52 $0 \cdot 56 \times 6$

54 $3 \cdot 95 \times 9$

Work out and give the remainder as a fraction.

55 $86 \div 6$

57 $389 \div 100$

56 $158 \div 9$

58 $160 \div 7$

Work out and give the remainder as a decimal.

59 $126 \div 10$

61 $67 \div 5$

60 $74 \div 4$

62 $190 \div 8$

63 Ai Ping has £3159 in her bank account. She withdraws £1374. How much is left in the account?

64 How many hours are there in December?

65 A box holds 16 tins. How many boxes can be filled from 360 tins? How many tins are left over?

66 There are 28 nails in each bag. How many nails are there in 35 bags?

A

Copy and complete.

1. 1·738 km = ☐ m
2. 27 m = ☐ km
3. 9 cm = ☐ m
4. 1·3 m = ☐ cm
5. 0·146 m = ☐ mm
6. 8 mm = ☐ cm
7. 0·7 m = ☐ cm
8. 395 m = ☐ km

9. 2·8 kg = ☐ g
10. 1500 kg = ☐ t
11. 368 g = ☐ kg
12. 5 t = ☐ kg

13. 2 litres = ☐ cl
14. 1·9 litres = ☐ ml
15. 50 ml = ☐ litres
16. 300 ml = ☐ cl

Work out the measurement shown by each arrow.

17.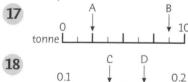

18.

19. 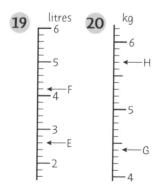 20.

B

21. 70 cl of wine is poured equally into 5 glasses. How much wine does each glass contain?

22. A ribbon is 1·8 m long. 137 mm is cut off. How long is the ribbon which is left?

23. A cyclist travels at 6 metres every second. How far will she cycle in 10 minutes in kilometres?

24. The 40 tins of tuna in a box weigh 10 kg. What does each tin weigh in grams?

For each shape work out:
a) the area
b) the perimeter.
(All lengths are in cm.)

25.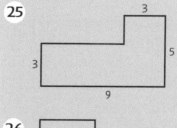

26.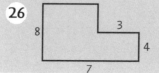

C

Copy and complete.

27. 85 years = ☐ decades
28. 91 days = ☐ weeks
29. 132 hours = ☐ days
30. 540 secs. = ☐ mins.

31. 1 day = ☐ minutes
32. 3 decades = ☐ months
33. 2 weeks = ☐ hours
34. 2 hours = ☐ seconds

35. What will be the date four weeks after:
a) October 15th
b) April 23rd
c) February 8th 2008
d) December 25th?

36. Turkey must be cooked for 40 minutes for every kilogram. Copy and complete the table.

WEIGHT	START	FINISH
5 kg	15:45	
6·5 kg	08:30	
9·5 kg	06:25	
7·5 kg	12:50	

37. The time in Tokyo is 9 hours ahead of the time in London. What is the time in Tokyo if the time in London is:
a) 08:00   b) 19:00?

Write the names of each of these 2-D shapes.

9 Which of the above shapes have:
   a) parallel lines
   b) perpendicular lines
   c) equal opposite angles
   d) equal adjacent angles?

Use squared paper.
Copy the shape and the mirror line and sketch the reflection.

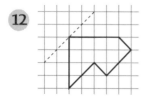

For each 3-D shape:
a) write its name
b) describe its flat faces.

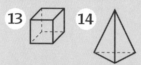

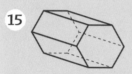

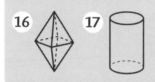

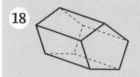

How many cubes are needed to build each shape?

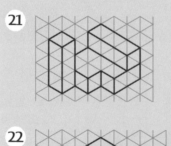

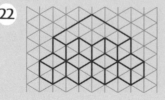

23 Copy the grid and the triangle.

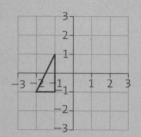

Translate the triangle:
a) Right 2, Up 2
b) Left 1, Down 2.

24 Copy the grid above. Plot these points and join them up in this order.
(0, 0) (0, 2) (1, 2) (1, 1) (3, 1) (3, 0) (0, 0)

Rotate the shape about (0, 0):
a) 90° clockwise
b) 180°.

Use a protractor.
Draw these angles.

25 76°   **27** 18°

26 143°   **28** 102°

Calculate the missing angles.

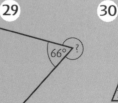

INTERPRETING DATA

For questions one to three find:
a) the range   c) the median
b) the mode   d) the mean.

1) The numbers of paintings completed each day by an artist.

3 1 0 2
3 4 0 1
2 4 1 5
0 1 3

2) The daily maximum temperatures recorded in one week in March.

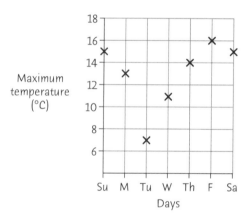

3) The numbers of shoes sold by a shop in each hour of trading.

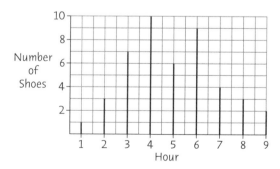

BAR CHARTS WITH GROUPED DATA

4) This bar chart shows the marks achieved by children in a test.

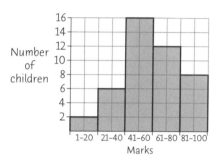

a) How many children scored between 41 and 60 marks?
b) How many children scored over 60 marks?
c) How many children took the test?

5) This bar chart shows the time taken by children to solve a problem.

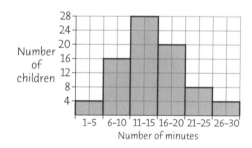

a) How many children took less than 11 minutes?
b) How many children took more than 20 minutes?
c) How many children altogether solved the problem?
d) What percentage of the children took more than 15 and less than 21 minutes?
e) What percentage of the children took less than 6 minutes?

PIE CHARTS

6 This pie chart shows how 72 people travelled to the same hotel.
Write down how many people travelled by:
a) train   b) car   c) plane.

7

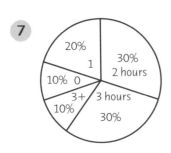

This pie chart shows the number of hours in one evening spent watching television by 40 children.

Copy and complete the table

HOURS	CHILDREN
0	
1	
2	
3	
3+	

CONVERSION GRAPHS

This graph converts Australian dollars to pounds.

8 Convert into pounds:

a) 140 dollars   d) 84 dollars
b) 28 dollars   e) 92 dollars
c) 100 dollars   f) 152 dollars

9 Convert into dollars:

a) £20   d) £40
b) £60   e) £16
c) £34   f) £25

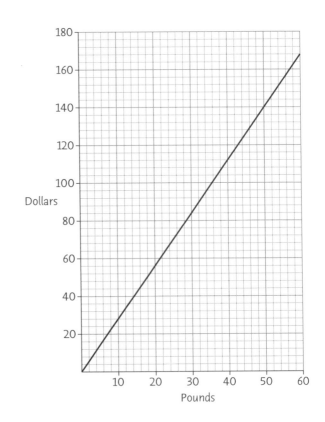

A

Find a pair of numbers with:

1 a sum of 14 and a product of 48.

2 a sum of 13 and a product of 22.

3 a sum of 17 and a product of 70.

4 a sum of 16 and a product of 48.

5 a sum of 16 and a product of 63.

6 a sum of 30 and a product of 125.

7 a sum of 17 and a product of 42.

8 a sum of 50 and a product of 600.

9 a sum of 21 and a product of 80.

10 a sum of 24 and a product of 144.

B

Find the number.

1 a 2-digit number
a prime number
the sum of its digits is 13

2 a 2-digit number
a multiple of both 3 and 4
the sum of its digits is 15

3 a prime number
a factor of 78
a 2-digit number

4 a 3-digit number
a square number
the product of its digits is 2

5 a multiple of 9
a 3-digit number below 200
the product of its digits is 16

6 a 2-digit number
a prime number
the product of its digits is 24

7 a square number
a 3-digit number
the product of its digits is 20

8 a 2-digit number
a factor of 184
a prime number

9 a multiple of 11
a multiple of 7
the product of its digits is 6

10 a 3-digit number
the sum of its digits is 9
a multiple of 37

C

Find two consecutive numbers with a product of:

1 552   3 702   5 812   7 1892   9 1722   11 4160

2 992   4 1122   6 1406   8 2256   10 2756   12 8010

Find a pair of any numbers with a product of:

13 115   15 287   17 395   19 671   21 493   23 851

14 111   16 143   18 201   20 623   22 949   24 1007

[You can't use '1' as one of the numbers!]

Copy and complete by writing the missing numbers in the boxes.

A

1. $(\square + 6) + 8 = 18$
2. $(\square - 6) \times 3 = 30$
3. $(\square \times 2) - 10 = 6$
4. $(\square \div 9) \div 1 = 9$

5. $(\square + 13) \div 3 = 7$
6. $(\square - 16) + 7 = 15$
7. $(\square \times 5) \times 8 = 80$
8. $(\square \div 7) - 2 = 7$

9. $(\square + 2) \times 6 = 36$
10. $(\square - 17) - 6 = 26$
11. $(\square \times 4) \div 2 = 8$
12. $(\square \div 3) + 11 = 17$

B

1.
```
  □ 4 □
+ 1 □ 8
-------
  4 1 4
```

2.
```
  5 □ 7
- □ 6 □
-------
  3 6 3
```

3.
```
      □ □ 9
   ×      4
----------
    1 3 9 □
```

4.
```
    8 7
3)2 □ 1
```

5.
```
  3 □ 3
+ □ 7 □
-------
  6 5 2
```

6.
```
  □ 6 □
- 2 □ 8
-------
  1 6 5
```

7.
```
    □ □ 7
  ×     6
--------
  3 1 6 □
```

8.
```
     4 8
6)2 □ 8
```

9.
```
  □ 3 □
+ 1 □ 5
-------
  6 8 3
```

10.
```
  8 □ 0
- □ 2 □
-------
  3 8 3
```

11.
```
    □ □ 5
  ×     9
--------
  2 5 6 □
```

12.
```
     5 4
9)4 □ 6
```

13.
```
  4 □ 5
+ □ 3 □
-------
  8 2 0
```

14.
```
  □ 3 □
- 1 □ 6
-------
  1 7 6
```

15.
```
    □ □ 6
  ×     7
--------
  1 6 5 □
```

16.
```
     9 6
6)5 □ 6
```

17.
```
  □ 9 □
+ 3 □ 7
-------
  7 0 1
```

18.
```
  6 □ 1
- □ 7 □
-------
  2 6 3
```

19.
```
    □ □ 6
  ×     3
--------
  2 4 4 □
```

20.
```
     7 7
4)3 □ 8
```

21.
```
  5 □ 9
+ □ 9 □
-------
  8 5 3
```

22.
```
  □ 2 □
- 4 □ 3
-------
  4 2 7
```

23.
```
    □ □ 2
  ×     8
--------
  2 8 1 □
```

24.
```
     6 5
8)5 □ 0
```

C

1. $\square 7 \times 1 \square = 611$
2. $3 \square \times \square 5 = 510$

3. $\square 8 \times 2 \square = 644$
4. $4 \square \times \square 8 = 1786$

5. $\square 4 \times 2 \square = 1512$
6. $3 \square \times \square 7 = 1221$

7.
```
    4 1 7
5)□ 0 □ 5
```

8.
```
    3 6 9
4)□ 4 □ 6
```

9.
```
    2 3 7
6)□ 4 □ 2
```

10.
```
    3 6 6
8)□ 9 □ 8
```

11.
```
    4 8 3
7)□ 3 □ 1
```

12.
```
    3 4 7
9)□ 1 □ 3
```